D1035515

Pushing the Numbers in Marketing

Pushing the Numbers in Marketing

A Real-World Guide to Essential Financial Analysis

David L. Rados

Q

Quorum Books

Westport, Connecticut / London

Library of Congress Cataloging-in-Publication Data

Rados, David L.
    Pushing the numbers in marketing : a real-world guide to essential
financial analysis / David L. Rados.
        p. cm.
    Includes index.
    ISBN 0-89930-736-1 (alk. paper)
    1. Marketing—Mathematics. 2. Marketing—Statistical methods.
3. Managerial accounting. 4. Managerial economics. I. Title.
HF5415.122.R33   1992
658.8'001'51—dc20   91-47643

British Library Cataloguing in Publication Data is available.

Library of Congress Catalog Card Number: 91-47643
ISBN: 0-89930-736-1

First published in 1992

Quorum Books, 88 Post Road West, Westport, CT 06881
An imprint of Greenwood Publishing Group, Inc.

Printed in the United States of America

The paper used in this book complies with the
Permanent Paper Standard issued by the National
Information Standards Organization (Z39.48-1984).

10 9 8 7 6 5 4 3 2 1

To Mildred and Jack
for much support and love over the years

Contents

Preface

This book is written for practicing marketers who want to improve their understanding of some useful but basic tools of financial analysis. It aims to help marketers and students of marketing master the elementary number crunching that marketers must do—cost analysis, contribution accounting, break-even points. Managers should buy the book, read it, and work through the problems by themselves. Teachers will find this book a good supplement or second text in executive workshops or MBA marketing courses. It is particularly well-suited for executive MBA classes where students want material they can use in their classes and on the job. Students should be warned that their professors will find the book "obvious" or "trivial" or "not worth a book." I have been around professors long enough to know that as far as managers and their interests are concerned these terms are compliments.

I have tried to make the book short, sweet, and clear. I have packed it with what I believe are examples and instances of the points I am trying to make.

The book contains a large number of problems and the answers to the problems. These are an important part of the book for readers who want to get the most from it.

I have tried—labored—to ensure that the numbers in the text, the problems, and the answers to the problems are correct. In particular, I believe that the answers to the elementary problems are all correct. As the slightly more difficult problems all involve some judgment or some guesswork, there can be no certain answers. But it is too much to expect of anyone to produce a book crammed with numbers and free of error. I will welcome comments and corrections in care of the publisher.

Several readers read one or more chapters and gave valuable suggestions and criticism, as did students in various executive MBA programs, in the United States, England, and Australia. A few were willing to have their names listed: Germain Böer, Mark Cohen, Jim Hartz, Marcus Van Amerigen, and Tony Zahorik. Frank Winslow scrutinized the manuscript and caught many errors and infelicities. Rachel Scott typed the manuscript and attended to countless other chores with tireless efficiency and good spirits. The reference librarians in the Walker Management Library were unfailingly helpful in tracking down facts, figures, spellings, and the sources of quotations.

Pushing the Numbers in Marketing

Chapter 1

First Words

Would you buy a book that promised to show you how to become an NFL coach by spending five minutes a day, to give you the five simple rules for composing great music, or to reveal the secrets you need to become a lawyer without spending three years in law school? You would not, because you know that coaching and the law require lengthy training and experience, and composing requires a good deal more.

Why then do so many people buy books that promise they can learn management in one minute or that give simple rules for making your first million? Both the authors and the readers must feel that there is not much to business, that just a secret here or a simple rule there is all that is needed. And best of all, according to these books, you can succeed in business without knowing any accounting or finance or marketing.

This is not such a book. I wrote this book because I had a problem, which to a professor means writing a book. I found that my consulting clients were often unable to do the simple number crunching that proves so useful in evaluating marketing proposals. Nor could executives in seminars or workshops. Even worse my students could not do it. It wasn't that the students hadn't studied such material; they had. They had all taken courses in microeconomics and accounting in which they were taught everything they needed. They had studied and passed their exams, but they didn't know simple number crunching and they couldn't do it. In the United States, we call this higher education.

The book reflects my belief that it is better to learn a few things well—really well—than to be exposed to many things.

I think of this book as being for the intelligent manager (or would-be manager), one who wants to keep on learning and is skeptical of books that promise too much. I can promise that you will learn a couple of useful tools and that you will pick up a smattering of economic theory along the way, but not more than a smattering.

The material in the book is not difficult. Some readers will already know a good deal of this material. They can expect to relearn it and understand it far better than they did. Most marketers, however, will not know the material, or will have half-learned it at some point, or will currently be using it but not quite understand what they are doing.

While the material is easy, the book has some depth for those who want to go deeper. It is packed with instances and examples that illustrate my points. There is a large collection of problems and questions at the back of the book, followed by the answers. To get the most out of the book, you should work the problems and answer the questions. You won't get them all. I'm not sure even I know all the answers.

The problems are divided into two classes: (1) Elementary problems require nothing more than application of material covered in the chapter that they follow. You should have no difficulties with these problems. (2) Slightly more difficult problems require you to bring to them some other information or approach than what is covered in the chapter. You may even have to make some shrewd guesses. What is in the chapter alone will not enable you to solve these slightly more difficult problems.

I recommend that you work a problem, look at the answer, work the next problem, look at the next answer, and so on. Once you start to read the answers you will discover that many are more than simply answers. Particularly with the slightly more difficult problems, I have tried to indicate how I thought about the problem.

WHAT YOU WILL FIND IN THIS BOOK

Woven through this book is a strand from economic theory. Although most readers will undoubtedly be familiar with economics, not all will. And, almost certainly, each reader knows less about economics than he thinks. Hence, Chapter 2 covers the preliminaries.

Economics of the sort likely to be useful to a manager is not all that hard to learn. The problems lie elsewhere—in the language economists use, in the aims of their profession, and in their general inability to speak plain English, a blemish unfortunately not confined to economists.

Here is what you will find in the rest of the book.

A discussion of costs—from the perspective of the manager and in the language of the accountant, and from the perspective of economics.

Marketing arithmetic—how retailers (and wholesalers) push the numbers, a topic that is easy to learn but that is essential for anyone who uses channels of distribution or who wants to understand how business works.

Averages and marginals—the difference between average cost and marginal cost, between an average anything and a marginal anything. This is important because of the usefulness of marginal thinking in business.

Marketing control statements—what contribution is and how it is used by marketers.

Break-even and just-cover points—what break-even is, why it is so important in marketing, why the professors laugh at people who use it, and how to bear their scorn.

Contribution analysis—how to look more deeply into the differences in contribution between what you plan and what you actually get.

Problems followed by answers to the problems.

Chapter 2

Why You Should Learn Some Economic Theory . . . but Only a Little

This chapter may seem a bit discourteous. I have some blunt things to say about microeconomics. But I would not have written this chapter—or this book—if I did not believe, based on my experience in consulting and in the classroom, that micro can help. The problem is that it helps, but not very much, which is what this chapter is about.

Before I tell you why you should learn some economics I have to explain what kind of economics I am talking about.

TWO DIVISIONS OF ECONOMICS

Economics divides into two broad areas, the big and the little. Macroeconomics deals with the economy as a whole, with questions of national import like unemployment, productivity, competitiveness, investment, governmental finance, and foreign trade. As such, it provides economists who would otherwise never touch the levers of power with the vicarious thrill of influencing the course of history. When the press refers to "economics," or when it illuminates the most recent errors made by economists in forecasting the economy, it refers to macroeconomics. All jokes about economists and economics prick the pretensions of macroeconomics.

Microeconomics studies the entities that make up the macroeconomic whole, such as consumers, businesses, industries, and markets; and it tries to understand how markets work, which to a microeconomist means understanding how prices work. Reflecting this emphasis on price, microeconomics is also called price theory. Because micro is more modest fare than macro, microeconomists live outside the public eye and hence are less subject to scorn. This book deals with only microeconomics. To keep this before the reader, I will always try to use the word *microeconomics* instead of *economics*.

LEARNING SOME MICROECONOMICS

Microeconomics underlies what this book is about. That means you will not just learn a tool or an approach; you will have some understanding of why the tool makes sense.

Well, why should you learn some microeconomics? Certainly not to impress your friends and astound your enemies. Certainly not to succeed in business or in life, or even to make money. All of the world's great fortunes have been amassed by people ignorant of microeconomics. Some of these rich people were so thoughtless that they made their pile before microeconomics was perfected in the modern age.

You should learn it so you will understand better how your business works and where the profits come from. You should learn it so this book will make more sense to you. And you should learn it because it can help you think through issues that arise elsewhere in your business or personal life.

You should learn only a little, because that's all you need to get the most out of this book and to progress in the field of marketing. And much of microeconomics, perhaps most of it, has no more relation to making things happen in business than organic chemistry has to grilling a steak.

The rest of this chapter tries to explain what microeconomics is, why it is so hard to use, and what its value is to a marketing manager.

Micro as a Description of the World

Microeconomics has value in two ways, as a description of the world and as a way of thinking about the world. Both raise difficulties.

The first question to ask of any description, particularly one that claims to be scientific, is, How good is it? (Or at a deeper level, Is it true?) Unfortunately it is not easy to say how good the descriptions of microeconomics are, or even to find discussions of the accuracy of its predictions.

We can contrast this perplexing situation with that faced by nineteenth-century physicists. They had found that light moved in waves and believed that waves needed some medium to move in. Can anyone imagine ripples moving across the surface of a pond that contains no water? The medium hypothesized to carry light waves was called "aether." It was a bizarre substance: weightless, perfectly transparent, capable of passing through a solid body like the earth, yet stiff enough to carry waves of light across the infinite distances of the universe. Aether did have some properties that could be tested, nevertheless; and when the classic experiment was done, in the 1880s, it conclusively demonstrated that there was no such thing. Physics has managed without aether ever since.

Where are the similar studies in microeconomics? One searches in vain for empirical work that settles an issue permanently. Instead when pressed for details, microeconomists tend to refer vaguely to some large, widespread body of evidence supporting the theory. Or if they are given to levity they argue that the theory of demand must be true, because if it weren't there would be a Nobel Prize for the economist who could prove it.

To avoid this discussion seeming too fanciful, note that microeconomics has its aether too. It is called utility. It is an emanation, invisible, indefinable, and, except in principle, immeasurable. It is this insensible substance, or conceit, that (subject to many qualifications) microeconomists imagine you and I maximize in making decisions.

Yet in spite of all this, there is something to microeconomics as a description of the world. It does catch roughly some of what goes on in business and in the economy, and it does provide some vague predictions as to what will happen when (say) prices fall or costs increase.

Micro as a Way of Thinking

The other general argument for microeconomics is that it offers a systematic way of approaching problems. It is, in an often-encountered phrase, "a way of thinking."

Sometimes, one even comes across the argument that even if the evidence for microeconomics were spotty and unconvincing, it would still have value as a way of thinking. This argument is substantially true, but it is unnerving, nevertheless.

For one thing, it suggests the kind of double-barreled argument lawyers sometimes advance in court: My client couldn't have killed the victim because she is afraid of guns and anyway was in Boston at the time, but if she did shoot him it was in self-defense. In the same way, the microeconomist says, Microeconomics provides good descriptions of the world, but even if it doesn't, it is still useful. More important, microeconomics purports to be a science. Should not a science offer more than a way of thinking? One expects reporters or cooks or postulants to develop ways of thinking. From a scientist, one expects ways of thinking and more.

Of course, its way of thinking is most suited for those problems where economic issues predominate, the everyday decisions made over and over again. Once other issues arise, as they do in important business decisions (and in important decisions elsewhere in life), the value of microeconomic analysis wanes, partly because the numbers put into an economic analysis are more uncertain, partly because important decisions raise questions of internal politics, power, motivation, and ethics that go far beyond the capacity or interests of the microeconomist.

WHY IS IT SO HARD TO USE MICROECONOMICS?

In spite of all its oddities and unsatisfactory conditions, microeconomics can give a manager a sense of power in analyzing problems. This is why microeconomics underlies a good deal of what is in this book. Unfortunately, it is far from easy to use microeconomics. There are three reasons why.

The First Difficulty—The Theory's Intent

Microeconomics does not intend to help a manager. It aims to explain the behavior of markets and market participants such as consumers and labor unions. Microeconomists see it as a science, not a business tool. The manager will find little in the textbooks to help decide how much to spend on advertising or how to respond to a competitor's price cut. Microeconomics is to business what organic chemistry is to cooking.

Take a typical problem facing a marketer who plans to introduce a new product. Among other things, a manager wants to know first, how much can be sold at several different prices for (say) the first few years following the introduction of the product; and second, how best to use this information? Microeconomists call the answer to the first question a demand schedule and the second they call a problem in profit maximization. The marketer does not know for sure what the demand schedule will be; and it is so difficult to judge sales at different prices that the final version will rarely have more than three or four prices in it.

The process whereby a marketer might estimate a future demand schedule is not central to the microeconomists's thinking. The microeconomist has little to say on such matters as how a manager might estimate a demand schedule, or how a manager might evaluate a demand schedule prepared by others. The microeconomist simply assumes that the demand schedule is already known.

The Second Difficulty—The Theory's Abstraction

The second reason that microeconomics is hard to use lies in its abstraction. Working with clear, simple ideas is the soul of rational thinking, and in fact much of the power of microeconomics lies in its dogged insistence on fundamentals, on only the most important features of the problems. But it is this very simplicity that keeps micro from being used, directly and easily, in business.

For one thing, microeconomists use the same words to describe their abstractions that you and I use to describe what we see around us; but when microeconomists use "firm" or "profit" or "perfect competition," they do not mean what you and I mean. Their "firm" is not the firm that you work for, or read about, or sell to; their "profit" is not what a firm reports at the end of the year, nor does it appear in the tax code, nor is it what is in the bank. Yet the words suggest otherwise. A simple proposition like "firms in perfect competition make zero profits" means nothing until one has laboriously tracked down the technical meanings of the three terms. Everyday words with technical meanings are a sure recipe for tripping up the unwary.

The microeconomist seems to carry the process of abstraction a long way. Were he an artist sketching a nude, he would produce a stick figure. As one example, imagine that the microeconomist wishes to study the output of a factory producing strawberry jam. You or I would say that the factory needs three major resources, machinery, workers, and raw materials like sugar and strawberries; but the microeconomist will represent in his equations that the factory's output is determined only by the amount of machinery and the number of workers. It is more useful to his theorizing to imagine that the factory can produce strawberry jam without any strawberries.

The ruthless abstraction of microeconomics also partially explains why microeconomists have so much trouble showing that the laws of microeconomics are true. Its laws are so hedged in by qualifications and special circumstances dictated by assumptions, that the practical man, the manager or politician, the diplomat or the bureaucrat, finds them difficult or impossible to use; and the microeconomist is hard pressed to show that what he knows is in fact true.

There is nothing wrong with abstraction per se. Quantum physicists spend much of their time working with probability waves in high-dimensional phase spaces, but unlike the waves on the surface of a pond, neither probability waves nor phase spaces are real. That is, they are not "out there." They are imaginary, existing only in minds of physicists. Yet this does not hamper their work. The problem with abstraction is how microeconomists use it. The process of solving a business problem goes something like this:

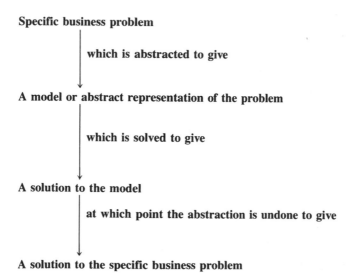

Specific business problem

   which is abstracted to give

A model or abstract representation of the problem

   which is solved to give

A solution to the model

   at which point the abstraction is undone to give

A solution to the specific business problem

The problem with abstraction, as used by microeconomists, is not that they stop with the solution of the abstract problem, but that they confuse the solution to the abstract problem with the solution to the business problem. How odd it seems to an outsider that microeconomists who stress the importance of reducing problems to their essentials never deal with the problem of putting the inessentials back in again. As a profession, microeconomics prefers to reason from the particular to the general, not from the general to the particular.

It is this oddity, this failure to undo the abstractions to deal with specifics, that is the second reason microeconomics is so hard to use. Here for example is how a microeconomist would reduce the recipe for jellied moose to its essence:

1. Pass the moose through a fine sieve.
2. Jell.
3. Unmold onto a very large platter, garnish, and serve.

This is not enough for the cooks of the world, nor does it help the Great Unwashed.

How then is one to apply microeconomics? One can not read a microeconomics textbook and apply what one finds there. Nor can one prudently approach a microeconomist and ask for help. The short answer to the question is, by becoming a microeconomist. This will ensure that you master the basic principles and that you believe. If you can not, or will not, then you must not expect to find any easy pickings in microeconomics. The gifted and experienced economist, William Baumol, sums it up like this:

I have never encountered a business problem in which my investigation was helped by any specific economic theorem, nor, may I add, have I ever met a practical problem in which I failed to be helped by the method of reasoning in the derivation of some economic theorem.[1]

There are two points here. First, nothing in the textbooks will help, but if you know enough to write textbooks, as Baumol has (and very good ones they are), if you have mastered the method of reasoning used by economists in proving theorems, you may find microeconomic theory useful. Second, it is not what the theorems contain, but the reasoning that is useful. As said earlier, microeconomics is useful as a way of thinking.

The Third Difficulty—The Theory's Generality

The third difficulty in applying microeconomic theory is the form that microeconomic predictions take.

The Theory Appears To Say More than It Actually Does. This can easily trip up the greenhorn. Take the law of demand, *the* great empirical regularity of economics. Stripped of its many qualifications, the law of demand says that changes in (real) prices oppose changes in demand: as the price goes up, the quantity demanded goes down. Unfortunately, that is all that it says. The law of demand says nothing about such pressing concerns as *when* the quantity will start to go down, *how fast* it will go down, or *how far* it will fall. Nor does it say anything about whether the answers for small increases in price differ from the answers for large increases in price.[2]

All this says is that the law of demand deals not with the relation between numbers—prices and quantities—as it appears to, but with directions. The law of demand is nothing more than this: as one goes up the other comes down. One up, the other down. All of the solid knowledge in microeconomics takes this character. One can expect a microeconomist to say whether and in what direction, but not how much, how soon, or how fast. The laws of microeconomics, such as they are, deal with qualities and directions, but not with numbers. This directional characteristic of microeconomics hints as to why it is so hard to say how well microeconomics describes the world.

The second example of the deceptively modest content of microeconomic theorizing concerns cartels.

Major premise:	Cartels are inherently, ineluctably doomed, as the theory of microeconomics indisputably proves.
Minor premise:	OPEC is a cartel.
Conclusion:	OPEC must eventually collapse.

The Organization of Petroleum Exporting Countries (OPEC) was founded in 1960, but until about 1973 it was relatively unimportant. Then in a few years, it managed to raise the price of oil from $1 a barrel to $30 a barrel, after which it overreached itself and the price fell. During these few years, between 1976 and 1981, OPEC was able to siphon off, from the United States alone, some $500 billion (in 1981 dollars), which Felix Rohatyn, the investment banker, has written was roughly half the value of all companies listed on the New York Stock Exchange.[3]

To which most microeconomists would say only, "Just wait. The theory is right. All cartels collapse eventually." The catch is in that "eventually." A casual reading says that a cartel can not stand and quickly collapses of its own instabilities. The prediction really says that a cartel must collapse, but that no one can say how soon or how fast. Nor is it the business of the microeconomist to point out that while a shrewd operator waits for the theoretical certainty to overtake him, he can get rich beyond dreams of greed. The prediction that cartels must collapse makes one think of the country saying—"We must have March sometime, if not in March."[4]

The first problem then is that microeconomic predictions appear to say more than they actually do, and hence can easily be misread.

Microeconomic Predictions Apply to Crowds but Not to the Individual. That is why one can not look closely into one's own behavior and find the laws of microeconomics. That is why your observation that *you* do not maximize profits in *your* business or that you did maximize your utility when you chose to marry will not engage the curiosity of a microeconomist.

That is to say, microeconomists almost always hedge their predictions with words like "tend to." This partly reflects the rudimentary state of microeconomic theory, but it does allow room for what could be a clear prediction to work out just the opposite.

Microeconomics Models the World, but a Model Is Not the World. Finally, just as the law of falling bodies deals with bodies falling in a vacuum, not bodies falling through air, or water, microeconomic predictions deal with abstract objects, not objects in the "real world," whatever that is. A microeconomic model is still only a model, it is not reality. It is easy to overlook this in trying to apply microeconomics.

Summary

These three problems with microeconomics—the theory's intent, its abstraction, and its seemingly misleading predictions—are not flaws in the theory. Anyone who knows the theory well understands its strengths and weaknesses, and what it says and what it doesn't say. It is the outsider who misreads, or misunderstands, or misuses the theory. The most common outsider is of course the student who, unwilling, has taken one required course in microeconomics and the manager who has taken none.

It is the modest aim of this book to teach the reader two ideas from microeconomics—cost theory and marginalism—in enough depth and enough detail to make them useful in reaching better marketing decisions.

WHAT MICROECONOMICS OFFERS TO A MANAGER AND WHAT IT DOESN'T OFFER

Microeconomics does not offer a great deal to a manager. But it does offer something, a *way of thinking*. Microeconomists may not know much—certainly not as much as, say, animal trainers or cellists know in their specialized areas—yet what they do know gives them a great deal of analytic power.

A way of thinking is not much, however, because thinking correctly requires a good deal of arduous training, and for one studying business, most of the time is spent studying microeconomic topics in which no potential businessman has the slightest interest. But without such training, one is sure to fall into a host of subtle and not-so-subtle errors. Fortunately, in marketing and the world of human behavior, one works with erroneous theory all the time and the theory that fashion dictates is correct this year will next year prove false. Errors are made, life goes on.

A way of thinking can provide two views of a problem. First, it can help arrive at rough guesses as to what is likely to happen when something else happens, rough guesses as to *whether* and *in what direction*. When oil prices first shot up in 1973, most politicians behaved as if drivers would continue to consume gasoline at the same rate, regardless. Microeconomists, on the other hand, working from first principles, predicted that (1) consumption would drop and (2) the drop would start small and then increase as time passed. (It is the mark of the pervasive public understanding of the basics of supply and demand that today practically the only class in society likely to make such an error is the politicians.)

The second value of a way of thinking is that it gives a manager a general method of attacking problems. It can help clarify problems, and organize and evaluate information; and it can help in comparing one course of action with another. There is a deep problem here, however, and that is in the relation between the *is* and the *should*. If microeconomics is a science and if it is true, as the microeconomists assure us it is, then firms already maximize profits, and any advice a managerial economist might offer about how to do things better is simply vain. One might as well try to instruct a tree how better to open its leaves to the sun. Botanists assure us that it is already doing the best it can.

This is a question that microeconomists never treat. We might guess at how they would defend themselves. Perhaps businesses do not simply maximize profits, but they maximize profits given the imperfect world in which we live, with all its imperfections, uncertainties, and luck. That is, given their ignorance of, say, the demand function and the marginal revenue product of labor. Unfortunately, maximizing profits given myriad limitations of the human being comes too close to "doing as well as one can under the circumstances." That, unfortunately, describes most of us most of the time, but it is an infirm basis for a science. Perhaps it is all in the difference between the mass and the individual. Microeconomics deals with groups, but advice given by the managerial economist is given to the individual firm. (Advice to governments is another matter.) Perhaps it is all a matter of language. Microeconomists assume that firms maximize profits; the maximization assumption lies at the very heart of their deductive system; the predictions they derive starting from the assumption of maximization of profits are, in their own view, overwhelmingly supported. But perhaps profit maximization is only a matter of speaking. "We pretend that firms behave *as if* they maximize, but we certainly don't believe that they do. It is just a convenient fiction, much like a legal fiction."

To an outsider all this seems unsatisfactory.

MANAGERIAL ECONOMICS

Having said all this about microeconomics and how little it offers to managers, I should point out that there is a corner of microeconomics that does intend to help businessmen. It is called managerial economics. It frankly takes ideas from microeconomics intended to describe the world as it is and fashions them into statements intended to prescribe the world, to say how things should be. That is, a microeconomist says, Businessmen maximize profits by setting marginal revenue equal to marginal costs. A managerial economist says, To maximize profits, managers should set marginal revenue equal to marginal cost.

Managerial economics is the poor cousin of microeconomics, attracting few resources and, in recent decades, none of the best microeconomic minds. But it is just what a manager wants. It aims to help the manager, and because it deals with managerial problems, it does not suffer from excessive abstraction. It still suffers from generality; that is, its prescriptions deal with general, not specific, problems. In other words, saying that a business should not spend more on its advertising than the advertising returns is solid, but not very helpful.

Managerial economics, then, offers some of the substance of microeconomics without some of its difficulties. And it is rooted in the crystal clear logic of the microeconomist. This books develops two of its ideas in some depth—what costs are and how to use them, and what the marginal principle is and how it is used, all as they apply to marketing, of course.

HOW TO USE MICROECONOMICS

1. Don't plan to learn very much. I believe there are at most half a dozen big microeconomic ideas that a manager should master. This book deals only with two of them—cost theory and marginal analysis.

2. Don't merely learn the key ideas. Master them. Keep at it until you understand them. This is just what this book aims to help you do.

3. If you want to learn more than you find in this inestimable book, don't study microeconomics at all. Go straight to managerial economics. It will be right up your alley.

NOTES

1. William Baumol, "What Can Economic Theory Contribute to Managerial Economics?" *American Economic Review,* Vol. 51, No. 2 (May 1961), 144.

2. And on a technical level, it says nothing about the type of mathematical representation that is most appropriate for its expression.

3. Felix Rohatyn, "Reconstructing America," *New York Review of Books,* March 5, 1981.

4. It also reminds one of Chairman Mao's comment when asked about the influence of the French revolution: "Too early to say." (For those educated in America, the French revolution began in 1789.)

Chapter 3

What Every Marketer Needs to Know About Costs

Cost means sacrifice. The cost of anything is what must be sacrificed to attain it. If there is no sacrifice, there is no cost.

It is enormously convenient to measure cost in monetary units, but it is not necessary. Cost has nothing to do with money. To a small boy with fifty cents to spend on a sweet, the cost of a candy bar is not fifty cents but the package of chocolate covered raisins he can not have. To my wife, the cost of a trip to Australia is not thousands of dollars but a long delay in redoing the kitchen. In addition, many sacrifices are difficult to value in dollars—such as the sacrifice of time, leisure, peace of mind, even life itself.

Other than in discussions of the fundamental nature of cost, the word *cost* by itself means nothing. We soon encounter deferred cost, expired cost, lost cost, utilized cost, product costs and period costs, direct costs and indirect costs, accounting costs, sunk costs, avoidable costs, opportunity costs, marginal costs, programmed costs, separable costs, attributable costs, traceable costs, historical costs—but never just cost.

One can not hope to apply economic cost concepts without recognizing that there are many kinds of cost. The word should therefore always be accompanied by a modifier. Students particularly should train themselves never to say "cost" without a modifier. It is a simple way to begin.

This chapter divides into two parts. The first deals with costs as seen by the manager and the accountant—variable, fixed, and programmed costs. In this section we talk the language of business. The second deals with costs as microeconomists think about them—marginal, sunk, and opportunity costs. The language here may look a bit strange but the ideas are important.

VARIABLE COSTS

These are costs that vary in proportion to small changes in activity. When variable costs are being discussed, they usually refer to costs that vary with changes in controllable activity. This is a roundabout way of saying that the very first question to answer is What do the variable costs vary with?

Let us look at some examples.

- Electric utilities have two kinds of variable costs: those that vary with the number of customers, such as costs of reading meters and costs of billing, and those that vary with the amount of electricity generated, such as fuel.

- Firms that produce groceries often use brokers to distribute their products. They pay brokers a commission on sales through the broker, a cost that varies with sales.

- Fees paid by franchisees are usually some percentage of gross sales. That's right, gross sales. A common figure is 8 percent. That's right, 8 percent.

- Insurance agents are paid a commission. State Farm's, for example, get 10 percent of auto insurance premiums and 15 percent of fire and casualty (which includes homeowners' and commercial policies). The agent receives these every year the policy is renewed. On life insurance the first-year commission is 30 to 50 percent with lesser percentages thereafter (down to 2 percent).[1]

Variable costs can vary with prices, as a salesman's commission. They can vary with sales, as do royalties and sales commissions. They can vary with volume of production, as do materials, labor, some indirect labor, shipping, and packaging. They can also vary with such things as the interest rate, the temperature, or the amount of overtime. The context will make things clear.

It can be difficult to identify in advance which costs will vary and how they will vary. Labor and material costs do not in themselves vary with production. They vary only if management makes them vary by using effective cost controls. Unless material is closely controlled, its use will increase faster than increases in production, particularly at high volume. Direct labor does not drop automatically as production does; employees will not lay themselves off, nor will they be diffident about spreading the work by slowing down. That is, direct labor varies with volume only if labor hours are adjusted as volume changes.

Variable costs are usually assumed by managers and accountants to be constant over wide ranges of output. There is no necessary reason why this should be so, however, and when large changes in production are being planned the assumption should be double checked. To question the assumption for small changes in output, however, as microeconomists sometimes do, is little more than affectation.

Variable cost is often called direct cost. This is too bad because the word *direct* suggests the cost can be traced to a product, and not all variable costs can be. But in language, usage is all.

How to Use Variable Costs

1. Make sure you have an estimate of variable costs of your product, brand, or whatever before you analyze a marketing decision.

2. Watch out for allocations of fixed costs that show up under variable costs. Calling a fixed cost variable doesn't make it variable.

FIXED COSTS

These costs don't change, in total, over a period of time, over some normal range of operations. These are important qualifications because few costs can be changed in the short run, say one day, and all costs can be changed in the long run, over years. Also, fixed costs may well increase if production increases sharply, say, from 60 to 95 percent of capacity.

Examples of fixed costs for a manufacturer would include depreciation of plant and equipment, real estate taxes, equipment leases, interest payments, most of the managerial and supervisory payroll, most of the costs of the maintenance crew.

Like variable costs, fixed costs do not exist in the absolute. Costs that appear to be given, to be beyond a manager's control, may turn out to be controllable, at least partially, under a different cost control system. If managers are not charged for office space, they will tend to use more of it. If the firm has the opportunity of renting part of its office space to outsiders and charges the foregone rent to the manager, that manager may well find it possible to reduce the space required.

What is fixed for one decision may be variable in another. The costs of running a sales branch are fixed for most day-to-day decisions concerning the sales force, but when consideration is given to closing or consolidating the branch these costs are no longer fixed. Such costs, that is, can not prudently be *assumed* to be fixed. If the decision is important enough, the assumption must be verified.

Fixed costs go by other names. They are non-variable costs to some, capacity costs to others. "Capacity" because regardless of how much business a firm does, there is a certain amount of expense that it must incur simply to be in business, to provide capacity. Fixed costs are sometimes called committed costs, which suggests that for the planning period under consideration they are unalterable.

How to Use Fixed Costs

Develop a healthy skepticism about the word *fixed*. It may be possible to find a way to un-fix them.

SEMI-VARIABLE COSTS

These costs mix variables and fixed costs and thus change as activity changes, but not in direct proportion. A salesman's pay combines salary, which does not vary with sales, and commission, which does.

			Percentage Increase
Sales	$600,000	$900,000	50
Salary	15,000	15,000	—
Commission @ 3%	18,000	27,000	50
Total pay	33,000	42,000	27

While sales have increased 50 percent, the salesman's pay has increased only 27 percent. Perhaps the best known example is the bachelor's hope that two can live as cheaply as one, that a one-bedroom apartment costs the same whether one person lives in it or two, that the cost of heating a home will increase only slightly when a second person arrives, and so on. While it is certain that two can not live as cheaply as one, the cost for two is not twice the cost for one, which characterizes semi-variable costs.

Semi-variable costs often increase in steps. For every ten salesmen, an additional sales supervisor is needed. For every additional $16 million in brand sales, one more brand assistant is needed.

PROGRAMMED COSTS

- Top tennis players get appearance money, often illicit, that can go as high as $250,000. If they play, they get the guarantee. If they finish in the money, they get the prize money on top of the appearance money.[2]

What kind of a cost is appearance money? It certainly isn't a variable cost. It doesn't vary with anything like attendance or television fees or ticket prices. It certainly isn't fixed. If the player fails to show, he is not paid.

- The brand manager for an adult health cereal plans to pack a bounce-back coupon in medium and large packages during a ten-week promotion at a cost of $1.1 million. This certainly isn't a fixed cost. The manager chose to run the promotion. Nor is it a variable cost. The promotion is budgeted at $1.1 million and doesn't vary with anything.

These are examples of programmed costs, costs that arise from management decisions and are associated with programs undertaken by management. Hence the word *programmed.*

Variable and semi-variable costs follow changes in production (or other activity), one closely tracking the changes, the other coming in fits and starts. Fixed costs do neither. Programmed costs do not follow changes in production (or other activity). In this, they are like fixed costs. But while in the short run, management has little control over fixed costs, programmed costs arise because management wills them. There is no necessity about programmed costs, as there is about fixed costs. All of the important costs under a marketer's control are programmed costs: costs of designing a new product, new product development, test marketing a new product, a sales contest for dealers, preparation and printing of a sales catalog, most advertising, and the planning and preparation required to set up a computerized marketing information system. As these examples show, most strategic marketing decisions give rise to programmed costs.

These examples illustrate another important fact about programmed costs. The relationship between what you spend and what you get is iffy. All too often, there is no practical way of deciding the lowest cost for a given output, or even the direction of change of cost that represents an improvement. There is no way, for example, to decide the lowest advertising budget needed to support sales or to decide whether one should cut or increase the budget. If he said it, John Wannamaker said it better: "I know half of my advertising is wasted, but I don't know which half." Nonprofit organizations face the same uncertainties. It is impossible to say how much an extra curator will add to a museum or an extra social worker will add to a burn center.

With production costs, there is at least a clear link between inputs and outputs, and one can safely say that less cost is better than more cost. With programmed costs, there are situations in which more is better, and others in which less is better; and it is usually impossible to tell which is which. There is another difference. Production costs are caused by sales and production. Programmed costs, particularly marketing programmed costs, aim to cause sales and production.

Moreover, programmed costs often come in indivisible units. A firm can send a display to a trade show, but it can not send half a display. Advertising must be inserted a minimum number of times in media to maintain continuity. There is a similar type of threshold with a salesman calling on an account. He must call a minimum number of times each year or risk losing the account all together. On the other hand, there is no necessary linear relationship. Sending two displays to a trade show will not double sales. Two ads, or two salesmen, may sell twice as much as one, or they may not. Here is one final example of the indivisibility of programmed costs: the average American film takes about two years to complete and costs around $30 million (in 1989). The $30 million is a programmed cost, the cost of the chip needed to play in the movie game. It hardly changes whether the film grosses one million or one hundred million.[3]

How to Use Programmed Costs

1. Don't make the mistake of thinking they are variable.
2. Don't make the mistake of thinking they are fixed. They are neither variable nor fixed.
3. Be sure you have identified the important programmed costs. They are the most important costs that the marketer controls.

AVOIDABLE COSTS

These are costs that have not been incurred but will be in the course of pursuing some action. Such costs come naturally to mind when a firm decides to do something it hasn't done before. When an activity is added, the added costs are avoidable costs. The firm *could* avoid these costs by not doing what it plans to do. Avoidable costs can also be thought of as costs that can be avoided by ceasing to do something and not doing anything else in its place. They occur when disinvestment occurs—a sales branch is closed, a product line dropped, or a division sold.

Whenever a policy is being considered which will involve "overhead expenditures" that could otherwise be avoided, they are part of the cost of that policy.[4]

Most people when they say that such and such costs so much are referring to avoidable costs. The opposite of avoidable costs is sunk costs. If there is anything characteristic of sunk costs it is their inevitability. And anything that is inevitable can not be avoided.

TRACEABLE COSTS

These are costs that can be assigned or traced to a source responsible for them—a person, a product, a customer segment, a reseller, a function, a department, a sales territory. They can be any of the costs already discussed.

They are sometimes called direct costs, in that there is a direct link between the cause of the cost and the cost. The opposite of traceable cost is common cost, a cost that can not clearly be linked with some cause.

The first four costs above—variable, fixed, semi-variable, and programmed—are the most useful to a manager. For many decisions, for most businesses, it is possible to re-classify costs recorded in the accounting system so as to get a better idea of the cost changes the decision is likely to create. In fact, merely dividing all costs into variable and programmed would probably improve the quality of most marketing decisions.

ACTUAL COSTS

This usually means historical cost, which is a stew of conjecture, opinion, and fact made by following a clear but arbitrary recipe. Even the term "historical" is a bit misleading, because costs not yet realized are inevitably included in historical costs, like estimates for future bad debts and depreciation of patents.

To an accountant, actual cost is a number arrived at by following Procedure. It is inevitably vague until one knows the Procedure that underlies it, and it is always arbitrary. There is no such thing as actual cost, as the reader will come to recognize.

To one who does not know accounting, actual cost means true cost, indisputable, ineluctable, absolute. "Historical costs have powerful sway over untutored minds," says one economist.[5] Certainly, actual cost does not mean higher precision, nor need it even be the correct costs. Most of the cost of an expensive lipstick is packaging, a cost clearly traceable to marketing, yet the packaging appears as a cost of manufacture. An order won on a promise of fast delivery may raise material and labor costs, which are avoidable and traceable to marketing, but which are recorded as manufacturing costs. The cost of on-the-job training is the production lost as experienced workers show trainees the ropes, and extra wear and tear on equipment; but both will show up not as training costs but as manufacturing costs.

Historical costs record what happened, after a fashion, but they are of little use in meeting management's needs when it comes to making decisions. They provide no base against which performance can be measured, either, and come, in any event, too late to correct inefficiencies. They provide no motivation for cost reduction, just as a cost-plus-fixed-fee contract provides none. They are of little use in budgeting for the future, although they are of some, and of no use in decision making, except that they can serve as a basis for forecasting future costs.

THE MIX OF COSTS

Develop a good understanding of the proportion of variable and fixed costs. It has a profound effect on the numbers, because variable costs are incurred near (or at) the time of the sale, and they are driven by the sale—

no sale, no variable costs. Even better, there is often time to use the revenues from the sale to pay for the variable costs. They often do not need to be financed. Fixed costs and programmed costs, on the other hand, are incurred well in advance of the time of sale, and they are often paid in advance as well.

Small firms tend to prefer variable cost methods of marketing because they do not need to tie up their financial resources in advance of the sale. Thus, they use (say) manufacturers representatives or brokers to sell their products instead of having their own sales force.

Now we turn to costs as seen by the microeconomist.

MARGINAL COSTS

This is the extra cost that results from the production of one extra unit. Marginal means on the fringes, away from the center. (Microeconomists often think of marginal cost as the cost of the very last item produced.)

Marginal cost is most easily seen in prime costs—labor, materials, packaging, freight. But they are not confined to such costs. An increase in *any* cost arising from the production of one more unit is part of the marginal cost of producing that unit. To emphasize this, some definitions of marginal cost are cast in terms of total cost: Marginal cost is the change in total cost that results from the production of one more unit.

In concept, marginal cost differs from variable cost. First, variable costs are *ex post,* while marginal costs are always *ex ante*. That is, variable costs look to the past, marginal costs look to the future. Second, variable costs are usually assumed to be constant over a wide range of output. In theory at least, marginal cost varies.[6] Third, variable costs are cash outlays. Marginal costs include non-cash costs, such as implicit costs and opportunity costs. Marginal cost is the change in total cost and may include extra wear and tear on machinery due to a rush order, extra risk of breakdowns, costs of bottlenecks, and so on. Finally there is a matter of language. There are short-run marginal costs and long-run marginal costs. There are no equivalent terms in accounting. Perhaps the closest would be variable cost for the short run and full cost for the long run.

SUNK COSTS

These are costs that are irrevocable in a given situation. They can be either costs that have already been spent or costs that will be the same regardless of which course is chosen. If the latter, there is no problem. They can be included in the arithmetic or omitted without affecting the *relative* preference for course A over course B. If the former, they are costs created by a decision made in the past that can not be changed by any decision that might be made in the future. A cost can become sunk even before any money passes hands. As soon as a cost can no longer be recalled, it is sunk.

The classic examples are investments in plant and equipment. Once a machine is installed its cost is sunk, and management can do only two things with it: use it or sell it. Using it will generate revenues; selling it will generate revenues. Since these revenues will occur in the future, it is not too late; they are still subject to modification, to control. But costs already spent can not be unspent or called back. Another example is the choice faced by the meat wholesaler: sell it or smell it.

This line of thinking gives rise to the Sunk Cost Principle: Because sunk costs can not be changed, ignore them in making a decision.

The admonition to ignore sunk costs is familiar to every business student, and is found in a number of folk sayings, which increases one's confidence in the soundness of the admonition:

Don't cry over spilt milk,

That's water over the dam,

Don't throw good money after bad.

The last is a rule for poker players ignored only by losers. Even Lady Macbeth understood, as when she tells Macbeth:

Things without all remedy should be without regard;
What's done is done. (III, ii)

Yet for all its powerful logic, sunk cost is not congenial to the human soul. It did not console Macbeth. Few people discover it on their own, and those who supposedly understand it often ignore it or misapply it. One takes to heart the advice not to cry over spilt milk for only the most trivial losses. The reader can expect vigorous argument in business on the question of including sunk costs with other costs relevant to a decision.

What is the cause of this apparently irrational behavior? Part of the explanation lies in the fact that senior managers may require consideration of sunk costs in a decision. Every manager has heard the argument: We've got to get those costs back. Even managers who know such considerations are not best for the firm may still believe that they are best for their departments and their careers.

A second reason is the realization that the sunk costs under consideration were once approved for what appeared to be sound reasons. Calling them sunk costs means classifying the decision as incorrect. It forces the mistake out into the open. Suppose, for example, a drug firm has spent over $12 million and four years trying to develop a form of insulin that can be implanted under the skin of a diabetic, thus freeing the diabetic for several months from the necessity of injecting himself with insulin. Suppose further that another $3 million is needed to finish development of the drug. The drug company is approached by a Swiss drug company, offering to sell it outright an equivalent product for $2 million. While it is clearly cheaper to buy than continue development, buying will call the soundness of the project into question.

Sunk costs often represent lost causes, then, and because they do, people sometimes hang on, refusing to recognize that the cause is lost. In the United States, lost causes give rise to litigation. For example, news reports told of a woman who lost $350,000 gambling in Las Vegas, surely a sunk cost if there ever was one. But not to the loser or rather to her lawyer; she sued the casinos, charging that they knew she lacked the capacity and capability to play blackjack properly but that they failed to suggest that she attend classes so that she could learn. Managers can not afford to think of sunk costs as microeconomists do. Sunk costs must be managed. Lee Iacocca felt he impressed Henry Ford by killing off the Cardinal, a small car Ford was considering building, because he was decisive enough to kill the project even after so much money had been spent on it.[7] Note the logic here. Recognizing sunk costs and dropping projects on which there are sizeable sunk costs are not the product of a disembodied, arid logic. Such acts are the stuff of high courage, at least of managerial courage.

One master in the use of sunk costs was Robert Moses, who built parks, bridges, highways, and dams in New York State. Moses learned early that once construction began, some way could be found to get the money to finish it. In building Jones Beach, for example, he planned two magnificent bathhouses costing $1 million each. All the legislature would begrudge him, however, was $150,000 for both (and for a water tower, as well).

Moses' architects told him to scale down his plans. He in turn told them to start construction on his million-dollar beauties. After he got the foundations down he ran out of money; whereupon he invited the legislators responsible for the parks down to Long Island to see his progress. When they arrived the foundations had been covered by the drifting sand and there was nothing to see.

What could the legislators do? Moses knew that they couldn't admit they had done a poor job of investigating the project. But why couldn't they simply deny him further funds? Because that would have meant the $150,000 had been utterly wasted. The force of those sunk costs got Moses his money, and in the course of a long career got him most of the projects that he wanted. As he said, "Once you sink that first stake, they'll never make you pull it up."[8] Moses knew more about sunk costs than the microeconomists.

Moses' strategy still works. It is alive and well in Washington, where it is the most common technique used by the Pentagon to purchase expensive weapons systems. Once spending starts, it is heavy work to stop it. They know how to use it in Hollywood, too, as the following quote from Director Jim Bridges suggests:

I was in the room on *Urban Cowboy* when Robert Evans said seriously to the studio that we could make the movie for eight million. The picture started going forward and we all knew it was going to cost twelve million, but that's a ploy. The idea is if you can get the studio pregnant enough, they can't pull out. It's not unusual. We did it on *China Syndrome* and everybody winked.[9]

Producers can also build on sunk costs before a film goes into production by getting the studio to begin paying for preproduction activities like scouting film sites or hiring an art director. The theory is pure Moses— the more money the studio puts into preproduction expenses the less likely it is to back out.[10]

Managers, therefore, must expect to lose many arguments concerning sunk cost. Sunk costs may still have some uses, nevertheless. If a firm spends $3 million developing a new product, this figure may give an order-of-magnitude estimate as to what competitors must spend to duplicate the development. It may, that is, give some indication of barriers to entry. Furthermore, in estimating what competitors will do, say, in setting a price, one may want to assume that the competitors will include sunk costs in their arithmetic. Finally it may be possible in many instances to fool governmental and regulatory bodies into approving higher prices by persuading the politicians on the board that sunk costs must be recovered.

How to Use Sunk Costs

1. Make sure you understand the logic underlying the sunk cost principle. Use the sunk cost principle in thinking about decisions, but don't make a big deal of what you are doing.

2. Don't expect anyone else to understand the sunk cost principle or to use it.

3. Don't expect to win any arguments using the sunk cost principle.

4. If you do try to argue the irrelevance of sunk costs, do it in terms of such hoary clichés as spilt milk or water over the dam. And if you do, do not expect this part of your argument to win converts. Thus, do not make it a major point, but only a minor point, one that you do not stress.

5. Since most people believe that sunk costs count, do not hesitate to gild your case with an (irrelevant) sunk cost argument. Thus, to what is already a solid argument, you might also add that so much money has already been spent that it makes a lot of economic sense to finish the job.

Once or twice in your career this line of argument will fail, because some one will catch you on the irrelevance of sunk costs. Do not be disheartened. For one thing, while some one person may understand sunk costs, few others will or will think the issue important. Moreover it is always possible to reword a fallacious argument to make it acceptable to some one who remembers his microeconomics. Simply say:

I misspoke when I said that we should go ahead *because* so much money has already been spent. What I should have said is that because so much money has already been spent, we won't have to spend much *more* to finish the job. We shouldn't stay in the race because most of the course is behind us, but because we are so near the finish.

Such a restatement will always enable you to wriggle out.

6. Above all, think. Do you want to spend *more?* If yes, fine. If not, don't let sunk costs dissuade you.

OPPORTUNITY COSTS

The opportunity cost of one alternative is the net cash flow of the best rejected alternative. It is, therefore, the value of an opportunity passed up, or foregone. To a supermarket there are two costs of taking on a new product: (1) an avoidable cost equal to the landed store cost of the item[11] and (2) an opportunity cost equal to the reduction in gross margin that results when shelf space is withdrawn from some existing item and devoted to the new one. If there were no shortage of shelf space, the supermarket would not have to forego any gross margin to add a new item, and therefore there would be no opportunity costs; which repeats the concept from the beginning of the chapter—no sacrifice means no cost.

Opportunity costs are created by scarcity.[12] Since there is no economics without scarcity it is hardly surprising that to microeconomists opportunity cost is *the* cost. When it is cash that is the scarce resource, opportunity cost is the same as the cash laid out for some factor of production. When it is the capacity of a resource that is scarce, opportunity cost is the correct cost. A firm hires a salesman. It appears that there is complete market access, and the cost of the salesman to the firm is the usual, avoidable items—salary, fringe benefits, travel expenses, moving and the like. What about recruitment expenses incurred to locate prospective salesmen? If the firm buys this recruitment service from an outside supplier, then the outlay cost is the correct cost; but if it does its own recruiting, the cost is the value foregone by using employees for recruiting instead of for the next best thing they could do. Similarly, selection and sales training are usually done by the firm's employees, and the scarce resource is not cash but their time and skills. Complete access to the market is almost never practical, and therefore opportunity cost enters into most economic calculations.

The Opportunity Cost of a Wrong Decision

One issue where opportunity costs come into their own is in exploring the consequences of a wrong decision. Imagine that there are two alternatives and two outcomes.

What You Find Out after the Fact

What you chose	A was the correct choice	B was the correct choice
Course A	Smiles	Frowns
Course B	Frowns	Smiles

The frowns are opportunity costs. If we choose A but it turns out that B was the better choice, we will have made a wrong decision. (Likewise if we choose B but A was the better choice.)

For example, the typical supermarket is presented with hundreds of new products every month. Yet important as new products are to a supermarket, the typical buyer spends only a minute or two evaluating each one. Shouldn't new products merit more careful consideration? No.

We can see this by considering the consequences of the two ways a new product decision can go bad. Suppose a buyer decides not to stock a new product that later turns out to be a good item. How will the buyer react? He will add the new product—later instead of sooner—and will be out-of-pocket the gross margin on one- or two-month's sales. The effect on the supermarket's bottom line will be virtually impossible to detect. That is, the opportunity cost of this wrong decision is low.

Suppose the buyer decides to stock a new product that later turns out to be a poor generator of gross margins. How will the buyer react? Sooner or later the product will show up as a poor producer. He will drop it or replace it with yet another new product, and will be out-of-pocket some gross margin on a few month's sales. Again the effect on the store's bottom line will be hard to detect. Again the opportunity cost of a wrong decision is low.

Now we know why buyers spend so little time evaluating new products. If the buyer makes either wrong decision, the consequences are slight. There is no point in spending more time and effort to do better.

The Opportunity Costs of Sales Promotion

Sales promotions can be evaluated on a number of criteria. One of these criteria deals with an opportunity cost.

An opportunity cost arises when customers who otherwise would have paid the regular retail price take advantage of a price pack or a coupon to buy at a discount. Let us say that the customer is brand loyal. She likes the brand, buys it regularly, and, in the absence of a promotion, she will pay the full price. Suppose we decide on a heavily discounted trial size as our promotion event. Common sense (as well as marketing research) says that brand loyal customers will have little interest in trial sizes—they buy the regular size or economy size—and hence the promotion will attract few who would otherwise pay full price. The opportunity costs of trial sizes are low.

A second possibility is a price pack, a package specially printed for the promotion with a discount price on it. If the price pack is the regular size (or the economy size), many brand loyal customers will find it on the shelves while they are shopping and buy it instead of their regular purchase. The opportunity costs of price packs are neither high nor low. They are moderate.

A third possibility is a coupon. Now the buyer can clip the coupon and use it when he next buys. He can adjust the timing of the purchase to meet his purchase cycle, and as a result he is likely to use the coupon to buy his normal supply at a discount. The opportunity costs of coupons are high.

Opportunity Costs Present Three Problems

Opportunity costs present three difficulties. The first is the presence of *implied alternatives*. I once lived across the street from a vegetable garden that occupied a plot of land worth about $35,000, on which zoning regulations permitted a house to be built. What was the cost to the gardener of the vegetables he grew? The cost of his time? "Not at all," he said. "I love gardening. I wouldn't work more than a forty-hour week if you paid me." Why doesn't he sell his lot and enjoy the proceeds? He could buy his vegetables from the greengrocer. (I was in Australia at the time.) "I guess you're right. I never thought of that." Although he does not consider selling, it is a possibility. Thus in such a situation, the microeconomist would say: "Well you may not realize it, but those vegetables of yours are costing you a lot more than you think. The cost is what you could buy with the income from $35,000 plus what you could earn with the time you spend in the garden."

Implied alternatives most often arise in marketing with decisions involving channels of distribution. Most firms that sell consumer products distribute them through middlemen, but they always have the possibility of going direct and capturing the middleman's margin themselves. For example,

	Use Retailers (000)	Distribute Direct to Customers (000)
Sales at retail	$200	$200
Retail gross margin	60	—
Sales at factory	140	200
Variable production costs	34	34
Contribution to overhead	106	166

By using retailers the firm forgoes extra revenues of $166,000 − $106,000 or $60,000. (It also avoids extra expenses, so the net difference will be much less than $60,000.)

The second difficulty arises from yet another form of opportunity costs: *imputed cost.* This is the opportunity cost of a factor of production that is not supplied by an outsider. Consider an engineer who sets up a company to manufacture a new hand-held laser "flashlight" that she has invented. At the end of the first year her income statement is:

Sales		$450,000
Variable cost of manufacture	$207,000	
Fixed cost of manufacture	81,000	288,000
Operating margin		162,000
Programmed marketing expenses	54,000	
General and administrative	81,000	135,000
Profit before tax		27,000

Into the business she has put her life savings of $45,000 and an inheritance of $155,000, and in addition, she has taken a cut in salary, paying herself $17,000 the first year, down from $34,000 the year before. Given this extra information, the engineer has had an unprofitable year.

Sales		$450,000
All avoidable expenses		423,000
Profit after avoidable expenses		27,000
Interest foregone on savings and inheritance	$ 13,000	
Salary foregone	17,000	30,000
Profit		(3,000)

Any small businessperson who can make an accounting profit in her first year is marked for bigger things. The point is that there is a cost to the factors the engineer contributed to her company—her capital and her labor—and these must be included in the total evaluation.

The last, and perhaps biggest, difficulty with opportunity costs arises from the fact that opportunity costs are easily overlooked. They do not show up on bank statements, income statements, or cash flow statements. At least they do not *appear* to show up on these statements. But they are there nevertheless. The bank balance, income statement, or cash flow statement would have been higher without them. The engineer in the previous paragraph is certainly out-of-pocket some $17,000, and the $17,000 is unquestionably cash.

To repeat, opportunity costs are easy to overlook. But they are real costs, and no manager can afford to neglect them. Here are two examples of situations where they existed but appeared invisible to the managers involved. They overlooked them and made poorer decisions as a result.

- In the 1960s Harry Sonneborn, president of McDonald's, set a limit of $50,000 on site acquisitions. As land values rose, the limit sometimes forced McDonald's to make deals on sites two or three blocks away from the best, but more expensive, sites. A broker who dealt with Sonneborn at the time said, "Harry looked only at the pure dollar cost of the real estate instead of lost income [from hamburger sales] by not making deals for more expensive property."[13] That is, Harry overlooked the opportunity cost of his spending limit.

- Fred Turner, who became president of McDonald's in 1969, preferred to buy land for McDonald's stores rather than lease it. A purchase might be more expensive at first, he reasoned, but eventually the land would be owned free and clear, while lease payments would go on forever and would increase as well. But owned assets give rise to imputed costs, which are opportunity costs. That is, McDonald's could either lease from a landlord or it could lease from itself. If it chose the landlord, it paid in the form of lease payments. If it leased from itself, it paid in the form of foregone income because it could always lease the property to someone else. This foregone income is easy to overlook. Turner did overlook it. In fact, it seemed so obvious to him that he had done the right thing that he called the decision "a no brainer."[14]

The strangest occasions involving opportunity costs are those involving either fully depreciated assets or assets valued at historic cost. Every astute manager knows that book values need not reflect market values. Yet not all managers are astute, and it is all too easy for those with little accounting background and no understanding of business to confuse book values with market values.

It is common for students to think of opportunity costs as indivisible costs, never variable. This is not the case. If a company produces a product that is not the most profitable it might have chosen, there is revenue foregone on every item it sells. If a salesman mistakenly spends his time selling a product with a gross contribution of $6 when he could just as easily sell one with a gross margin of $9, each unit sold has an opportunity cost of $3.

Some depreciation may be opportunity cost. Two forces contribute to depreciation, time and use. Some things, like a painting or a warehouse, wear out through the passage of time. Use has little effect. Other things like a mine wear out through use, and time has little effect. Still others, like conveyor belts and automobiles, are affected by both. Use depreciation involves opportunity costs, because what one uses today is not available for use tomorrow. Jam today means less jam tomorrow, just as extracting ore from a mine today shortens the mine's life. This even applies to a resource that can be renewed, such as a forest.

How To Use Opportunity Costs

1. Be on the lookout for opportunity costs. Ask often, What else could I be doing with this money and these resources? When I choose course A instead of course B, what am I giving up?

2. Beware of the hidden costs of assets that you own—like fully depreciated assets. They are not free. They could be used in other ways that might generate cash. That foregone cash is the cost of using owned assets. (Think, for example, of your investment in your home.)

3. Be alert for managers like Sonneborn and Turner. You may be able to exploit their ignorance.

HOW TO CLASSIFY COSTS

The marketer then must get good at classifying costs into fixed, variable, and programmed. There are three ways to do this:

1. Use your own business judgment.
2. Talk to someone who knows how your costs behave.
3. Use formal tools to do the job.

Using your own judgment is by far the most important. First, classifying costs does not take a great deal of time, because most of the issues that call for cost classification arise over and over. That is, once a cost is classified as varying with sales, it need not be reclassified until something about the cost or about sales changes. Second, getting the right classification is important enough to merit the attention of a senior manager. Third, the manager usually knows enough about the costs and how they are incurred to classify them correctly.

But there will be occasions when help is needed—perhaps to classify an unfamiliar cost, to assess what a cost may do in the future, or to judge how a familiar cost may respond to unfamiliar circumstances. In such circumstances, it can be worthwhile to ask an expert.

The expert will usually be a cost accountant or a cost analyst. Under appropriate questioning, they will reveal what they know. As always the key question is, As this activity increases, what is likely to happen to that cost?

There are, in addition, formal tools of analysis that can be used to judge the behavior of costs. These tools do not enjoy widespread use, however. They are tricky to use, the information they work on is not typically on hand, and they illuminate last year's behavior when what one wants is next year's. Still, they play a modest role.

An Example: Classifying a Publisher's Costs

Let us look at the production costs incurred by a book publisher. Here are sixteen such costs with some discussion of the nature of each.[15]

1. Paper and ink	Varies with the size of the print order.
2. Labor to run the printing press	Probably varies with the size of the print order, but this depends on the contract with the union and the firm's employment practices. As a first approximation, treat labor costs as variable.
3. Printing the book jackets	Varies with the print order.
4. Binders' boards	Varies with the number of volumes bound, which need not equal the number printed.
5. Binding labor	The same as item 4.
6. Miscellaneous, such as shipping boxes and supplies	Varies with print order.
7. Composition	Varies with length and difficulty of book. A one-time cost. Treat as programmed.
8. Alterations in type due either to errors or changes by the author	Varies with number of errors and changes. Treat as programmed.
9. Press set-up	Programmed. This and the next three are all one-time costs.
10. Further presswork for illustrations, charts, multicolor jackets, and the like	Programmed.
11. Binders' dies	Programmed.

12. Binding set-up	Programmed.
13. Amortization of plates	Non-cash cost that varies with print order.
14. Spoilage of sheets and bound books	Programmed. But may increase a little for books with longer print orders. So it is variable?
15. Copyright fees	Programmed.
16. Royalties	Vary with the number of copies sold, not the number of copies printed; but the usual contract makes these semi-variable, that is, 7 percent of the actual cash received by the publisher for the first five hundred copies, 10 percent for the next thousand copies, and 14 percent thereafter.

An Example: Classifying a String Quartet's Costs

The table contains an operating statement for a string quartet, which we can call The Quartet. We want to classify the costs to better understand the financial consequences of adding concerts. That is, we are interested in how costs change as The Quartet decides to add a few extra concerts or decides to cut back by a few.

Operating Statement for a String Quartet

Concert	$100,000		36.0%
Residencies	164,000		59.1
Unearned income	8,000		2.9
Recordings and videos	5,500		2.0
Reimbursements			
Total Income		$277,500	100.0%
Road expenses			
Air travel	30,000		10.8
Train travel			
Car or taxi	9,900		3.6
Hotels	10,000		3.6
Meals	7,000		2.5
Total road expenses		56,900	20.5
General expenses			
Telephone	2,000		0.7
Advertising*	3,000		1.1

Gifts	500	0.2	
Business meals	2,800	1.0	
Recordings and tapes	200	0.1	
Postage	375	0.1	
Music	650	0.2	
Accounting and legal	3,000	1.1	
Supplies	350	0.1	
Union dues	400	0.1	
Total general expenses		13,275	4.8
Management fees			
Commissions	17,000	6.1	
Advertising	2,300	0.8	
Postage	600	0.2	
Telephone	500	0.2	
Photos	500	0.2	
Printing	2,300	0.8	
Tapes and recordings	375	0.1	
Foreign commissions	3,500	1.3	
Other			
Total management fees		27,075	9.8
Publicist			
Fee	12,000	4.3	
Postage	1,200	0.4	
Telephone and telex	600	0.2	
Printing	1,200	0.4	
Commission			
Total publicist expenses		15,000	5.4
Total expenses		112,250	40.5
Net income before taxes		165,250	59.5
Net income per player		41,313	14.9

*Includes both advertising and publicity.

Source: David M. Rubin, "Six quartets in search of an auditor," *Chamber Music* (Fall 1989), 17.

Income

- Concert fees will vary with the number of concerts. All other income is fixed in the short run—say, for the next year.

Costs

- Road expenses vary with the number of concerts. But just how they vary is hard to say.

General Expenses

- Telephone probably increases with the number of concerts, but not by much.

- Advertising is probably fixed. (The promoter typically pays for local ads.)
- Gifts. Gifts? What gifts does a string quartet give, and to whom? This is probably a programmed cost. It will not vary with the number of concerts.
- Business meals. Probably varies a little with the number of concerts.
- Postage. Mostly programmed, but may vary a little.
- Music. Programmed.
- Accounting, legal, and supplies. Mostly fixed in any given year.
- Union dues. Fixed.

Management Fees

- Commissions. Vary with concert fees, which vary with the number of concerts.
- Advertising. Probably programmed.
- Postage, telephone. Varies a little with the number of concerts.
- Photos. Programmed.
- Printing. Hard to say. What is being printed? Probably this cost does not vary with the number of concerts.
- Tapes and recordings. Programmed.
- Foreign commissions. Varies only with number of foreign concerts.

Publicist

- Fees. Programmed. Certainly not fixed.
- Other expenses. Probably vary a little with number of concerts.

Note that there is a fair amount of guessing in this process, but only because the serious music business is unknown territory. With other, more familiar products, there is less guessing. And on their own home ground, most managers should be able to classify most costs accurately the first time around.

SUMMARY

There are a great many cost categories, from the point of view of the manager and from the point of view of the microeconomist. And there are even more that have not been discussed in this chapter, such as full costs, fully distributed cost, fully allocated cost, and absorption cost. In specific situations, the manager must be sure to get the exact meaning of the terms used. This is usually a matter of asking questions of cost analysts, accountants, and others in a position to know.

But without question, the three most important costs for the marketer are (1) variable costs, (2) fixed costs, and (3) programmed costs.

NOTES

1. Carol J. Loomis, "State Farm Is Off the Charts," *Fortune* (April 8, 1991), 79. This generates average commissions of around $150,000 a year before expenses, and $90,000 a year after—not riches but a comfortable living for most.

2. For a discussion of this and other matters see John Feinstein's *Hard Courts* (New York: Villard Books, 1991).

3. "Entertainment Industry," *The Economist,* December 23, 1990, 4.

4. J. M. Clark, *Studies in the Economics of Overhead Costs* (Chicago: University of Chicago Press, 1923), 21.

5. George J. Stigler, *The Theory of Price* (New York: Macmillan, 1966), 104.

6. The evidence on this point, which is hotly debated, seems to indicate that marginal costs are typically constant over wide ranges as well.

7. David Halberstam, *The Reckoning* (New York: William Morrow & Co., 1986), 362.

8. Robert Caro, *The Power Broker: Robert Moses and the Fall of New York* (New York: Knopf, 1974), 218–225.

9. Mark Litwak, *Reel Power* (New York: William Morrow & Co., 1986), 162.

10. Litwak, *Reel Power,* 79.

11. Landed store cost is the invoice price less discounts plus inbound freight.

12. A classic discussion of opportunity costs is R. H. Coase's."The Nature of Cost," reprinted in David Solomon, ed., *Studies in Cost Analysis* (London: Sweet and Maxwell, 1968), 118–133.

13. John F. Love, *McDonald's: Behind the Arches* (New York: Bantam Books, 1986), 238.

14. Love, *McDonald's,* 283.

15. Gordon F. Boals, "An Economic Analysis of Book Publishing," unpublished Ph.D. dissertation (Princeton, N.J.: Princeton University, 1970), 47–48.

Chapter 4

Elements of Marketing Arithmetic

This chapter introduces the simple commercial arithmetic necessary to analyze marketing problems.

GROSS MARGINS

Margin is the difference between a product's cost and its price. Most retailers and wholesalers determine prices by a cost-plus method in which a certain percentage of the product's cost—invoice cost plus freight charges minus discounts for prompt payment—is added to the cost to give a final price. But although prices are calculated on the basis of costs, they are commonly quoted as a percentage of selling price. Thus, a product costing a retailer eight cents and selling for a dime is said to carry a margin of 20 percent, not 25 percent. The difference between a product's cost and its price is called variously margin, gross margin, markup, and markon. The reader can expect to encounter all these terms and more.

Suppose a men's clothing store buys a suit for $165. Using margins typical in the men's garment trade, the retailer would price the suit at about $274. What is the markup? In dollars it is $274 − $165 = $109. In percentages it is about 66 percent on cost, and 109/274 = 0.4, or 40 percent on selling price. It is the latter figure, the markup on selling price, that is used in business courses, in the business press, and in business. Markup (or markon or margin) is quoted as a percentage of selling price.

The typical margin on men's suits is 40 percent. The retailer, that is, will normally take a 40 percent margin on suits. If he pays $195 what price must he set? Let

C = cost paid to the supplier, in dollars
P = selling price to be set, in dollars
M = margin, as a percentage of selling price

Then,

$$P = C + (P \times M)$$

$$P - P \times M = C$$

$$P(1 - M) = C$$

$$P = \frac{C}{1 - M}$$

Since $C = \$195$ and $M = 0.40$,

$$P = \frac{195}{1 - 0.4} = \frac{195}{0.6} = \$325.00$$

Mechanically applying the 40-percent margin indicates the suit's price should be $325.00. This may be an acceptable price, or the retailer may adjust it to one more conventional in his business, perhaps $320, $319.95, or $329.95.

Clearly, percentage margin on selling price is related to percentage margin on cost. In some few situations, it is useful to convert from one to the other. The following formulas perform this simple conversion.

$$\% \text{ Margin on price} = \frac{\% \text{ Margin on cost}}{100\% + \% \text{ Margin on cost}}$$

$$\% \text{ Margin on cost} = \frac{\% \text{ Margin on price}}{100\% - \% \text{ Margin on price}}$$

Memorizing such formulas is pointless. But you should be able to derive them. This is so easy to do that it does not bear discussion.

A typical product made by a manufacturer is sold to a wholesaler who resells it to a retailer who resells it to a consumer. Each of these parties adopts the same convention: each computes his margin as a percentage of his selling price. Let us say the manufacturer produces an item for the cost of $192 and adds to the cost a profit margin of $48. This means the wholesaler must pay $192 + \$48 = \$240$. What is the manufacturer's margin?

$$P = C + P \times M$$

$$M = \frac{P - C}{P} = 1 - \frac{C}{P}$$

$$= \frac{240 - 192}{240} = 1 - 0.8 = 0.2 \text{ (or 20\%)}$$

The wholesaler resells the item to a retailer for $300. The wholesaler's margin is

$$M = \frac{P - C}{P} = 0.2 \text{ (or 20\%)}$$

The retailer takes a 45-percent margin. What price does he set?

$$P = \frac{C}{1 - M} = \frac{\$300}{1 - 0.45} = \$545$$

Note that the manufacturer's price becomes the wholesaler's cost, and the wholesaler's price becomes the retailer's cost.

Discounts and Chain Discounts

Manufacturers often suggest the price at which a product should be sold by a retailer. If the manufacturer suggests a retail price of $120 while selling the item to the retailer for $72, the manufacturer is, in effect, suggesting a retail margin of 40 percent. The customary way of saying this is that the manufacturer offers a "trade discount" of 40 percent. If the retailer chooses to sell the item for, say, $110 instead of $120, the retailer will still have to pay "$120 less 40 percent," or $72, and hence take a lower gross margin.

Occasionally, discounts from a suggested resale price are computed in two or more steps. For example, a manufacturer might offer discounts of 40 percent and 5 percent on a product priced to be resold at $120. This means that in addition to the original discount (suggested margin) of 40 percent (i.e., $48), the manufacturer has allowed an additional 5 percent. This does not mean 40 percent plus 5 percent, however; it means $120 less 40 percent of $120, less 5 percent of $120 less 40 percent of $120. Thus the retailer pays

Suggested retail price	$120.00	100%	
Less 40% discount	48.00	40	
	72.00	60	100%
Less additional 5%	3.60	3	5
Price retailer pays	68.40	57	95

The 40 percent and 5 percent is called a chain discount, because the discounts are chained together. In chain discounts, the specific percentage link in the chain that is referred to (say, 5 percent, as in the present example) is calculated on the price that is derived after the application of the prior link or links to the suggested retail price. This rather cumbersome practice of stating discounts (or margins) probably arose originally to advise customers of changes in a discount structure, but over the years in certain industries it has become traditional.

When a manufacturer sells to a wholesaler or distributor, who in turn sells to a retailer, prices are generally listed as discounts from a suggested retail price. A product suggested to sell for $120 at retail, with a suggested retail margin of 40 percent and a suggested wholesale margin of 20 percent, will be sold by the wholesaler to the retailer at a price of $72 ($120 less 40 percent) and will be sold by the manufacturer to the wholesaler for $57.60 ($72 less 20 percent). Once again, the margin for a particular institution in the channel of distribution is quoted as a percentage of the price at which the institution sells.

Terms of Sale

Terms of sale set forth in brief are the conditions under which a company offers to sell its goods or services. They include, in addition to price, a statement of trade discounts, the date by which the amount is to be paid, and shipping responsibilities.

For example, terms of sale of "$50 per unit, 2/10 e.o.m., 60 days net, f.o.b. seller's plant" indicate that (1) the price is $50; (2) a 2-percent trade discount off the invoice price (i.e., $1) will be offered if the invoice is paid within a period ending ten days after the end of the month in which the invoice is issued; (3) if no discount is taken, the total amount is due within sixty days of the invoice date, and (4) the title and responsibility for freight pass to the buyer at the seller's plant. Note that this example does not show how cash discounts work, but rather how they are supposed to work. Many customers, particularly important ones, take the discount even if they do not pay on time, treating it as little more than a price concession.

Here, the letters e.o.m. stand for "end of month." In their absence, to qualify for the 2-percent discount the buyer would have to pay within ten days of the date on the invoice. The letters f.o.b. stand for "free on board," meaning that the seller will load the goods onto a truck (or boxcar or what have you) at no extra charge, but that from that point on, the cost of shipping and responsibility for damage pass to the buyer. While these are just two of many different discount and shipping terms, they are perhaps the ones most commonly used in business today.

Here are two examples of terms of sale. Traditionally, the women's apparel industry offers retailers an 8-percent discount on bills paid within ten days of the beginning of the month following shipment of the goods. The carpet industry traditionally grants its retailers 5/10 e.o.m.

Costs of Distribution

The difference between the manufacturer's price and the retailer's price can be considered the cost of distribution. Return to the item with a recommended retail price of $120, a retail margin of 40 percent, and a wholesale margin of 20 percent. In this case, the cost of distribution is $48 to the retailer and $14.40 to the wholesaler, a total of $62.40, or 48 percent of the retail selling price, a typical figure. This $62.40 may be considered the fee the manufacturer must pay the wholesaler and retailer to distribute his products. The manufacturer does not have to use such middlemen. If he chooses, he can sell directly to the consumer, perhaps by mail, door-to-door, telephone, or through his own retail stores; if he does he can charge the same price any other retailer does, $120, and capture the $62.40 himself. If he does use distributors, he incurs a cost, in the form of lost revenue, to have middlemen distribute for him. This is the cost of distribution.

Margins in Practice

The size of a margin is usually determined by traditional practice in the trade. Thus a jeweler pricing a diamond, a baker a tart, a street vendor a pennant, and a boat dealer a cabin cruiser all apply more or less mechanically margins conventional in their trades. Some retailers and wholesalers in fact use the same margin for all their goods, a procedure of refreshing simplicity.[1] Most, however, use different markups for different classes of merchandise and under different competitive conditions. Retail gross margins vary widely among different retail trades and within department stores and supermarkets. Some typical figures follow.

Approximate Gross Margins for Selected Retail Trades

Gross Margin Range	Retail Trades
50% or more	Custom tailors, monuments, florists and nurseries, bakery shops, and furs
40%–50%	Garages, jewelry, restaurants, eating places, furniture, and undertaking
35%–40%	Musical instruments, house furnishing, dairy and poultry products, gifts, novelties, souvenirs, books, furniture, drinking places, taverns, bars, office equipment and supplies, floor coverings, shoes (family stores), and electric and gas household appliances
20%–30%	Hardware, sporting goods, dry goods, general merchandise, lumber, cigar stores and stands, filling stations, meats, hardware, and farm implements
Below 20%	Alcoholic beverage package stores, motor vehicles, groceries, and meats

Source: Dun & Bradstreet.

Typical Gross Margins in Supermarkets Representative Grocery Margins (for independent supermarkets)

TOTAL STORE	21.6%
Meat	21.3
Produce	30.1
Dairy	14.2
Bakery	26.2

Frozen foods—total	25.2%	Detergents	14.9%
Baby foods	14.0	Canned meat	21.0
Beer	14.7	Paper products	26.6
Candy	26.8	Pickles, olives	29.4
Coffee, tea, cocoa	9.0	Salt, seasonings	30.8
Canned fish	21.5	Sugar	12.0
Household supplies	31.4	Total non-foods	27.9
Jams, jellies, spreads	24.0	Health and beauty aids	29.2
Macaroni and pasta	23.3	Housewares	24.5

Source: *Progressive Grocer* (April 1968), 91.

Typical Gross Margin Ranges in Drug Stores

Prescriptions	35–40%
Drugs/proprietaries	30–35
Toiletries	25–30
Cosmetics	35–40
Stationery	40–45
Tobacco	15–20
Candy	25–30
Housewares	35–45
Toys	35–40
Photo	20–25
General merchandise	35–45
Do-it-yourself	35–45
Grocery/liquor	15–20
Misc./promotional	15–20

Source: *Drug Store News* (May 4, 1981).

Supermarket Gross Margins by Product Class

Baby foods	9.6%
Coffee	11.8
Soft drinks and mixes	18.3

Baking needs	18.4	
Dressings	19.0	
Bakery foods	20.4	
Breakfast foods	21.2	
Beer and wine	21.9	
Canned and dry soup	21.9	
Canned fish	22.0	
Canned juice	22.4	
Canned vegetables	22.6	
Canned fruit	23.1	
Tea	23.2	
Syrups	23.6	
Spreads	23.6	
Desserts and toppings	23.9	
Cookies and crackers	24.1	
Sauces	24.1	
Canned meat and specialty foods	24.3	
Pasta	25.8	
Dried vegetables	26.2	
Diet and low-calorie foods	26.8	
Pickles and relishes	28.1	
Nuts	28.5	
Snacks	29.2	
Dried fruits	29.2	
Olives and vinegar	29.9	
Candy and gum	32.4	
Spices and extracts	37.0	
Total grocery		21.9%
Tobacco products	14.2	
Soaps and detergents	18.7	
Paper, plastic, film and foil	20.5	
Laundry and ironing aids	21.6	
Pet foods	22.2	
Cleansers	25.8	
Waxes and polishes	30.1	
Misc. household supplies	31.0	
Total non-foods		19.4
Meat	20.6	
Dairy products	24.3	
Delicatessen	27.0	
Frozen foods	31.9	
Produce	32.5	
Total perishables		25.5
General merchandise	37.0	
Health and beauty aids	26.8	
All other	25.3	
Total supermarket		24.1

Source: *Progressive Grocer* (July 1984), 42.

Price Lining

Margin (plus turnover, which is discussed below) dominates the thinking of retailers and wholesalers in the area of price. One example is the practice called "price lining." A price line is a retail price that is unchanged over long periods of time. Rather than buy merchandise and mark it up to get some price, the retailer starts with the desired retail price and works backward, searching for merchandise that can be sold at that price, which will give the customary gross margin. The original F. W. Woolworth stores sold merchandise at two price lines, a nickel and a dime, hence the name, now of historic interest only, "the five and dime." The practice is widely used by department stores in pricing dresses, sheets, gloves, blouses, skirts, and the like. At one time New York City had a chain of "69 cent shops" in which each of the four thousand items carried sold at 69 cents; and North Carolina has a chain of stores called "Everything for a Dollar."

The importance of maintaining the price line is seen by market adjustments to increased production costs. Two basic actions are possible, pass the increase along by raising prices or reduce quality. Under price lining, quality is reduced. For example, retailers once sold women's gloves at two price lines, $2 and $3, for which they paid at wholesale $12.50 to $14.50 per dozen and $18.00 to $21.00 per dozen, respectively. If cost increases forced a new price of $16.00 per dozen, retailers would see them as too expensive to be sold at $2.00 and too cheap to sell at $3. The wholesaler in this situation would either try to get $18 per dozen for the gloves or would drop the line. The manufacturer, of course, would avoid putting the wholesaler in such a situation and cheapen the gloves so they could be sold for less than $14.50. This preserved the retailer's "price lines."

Price lining usually reflects consumers' expectations: they have been led over time to expect merchandise only at the price points, and they continue to do so. Price lining would not be of importance to retailers if consumers did not expect to find them and respond favorably to their existence.

Turnover

To the concept of margin we must add that of turnover. A 50-percent margin may be far less profitable than a 10-percent one if far fewer items are sold at the 50-percent margin. Turnover is the number of times the average inventory in an item is sold during the year. There are three methods of calculating turnover (or stockturn, as it is also called), all usually giving about the same result.

$$a. \quad \frac{\text{Net sales}}{\text{Average inventory (at retail)}}$$

b. $\dfrac{\text{Number of units sold}}{\text{Average inventory (in units)}}$

c. $\dfrac{\text{Cost of goods sold}}{\text{Average inventory (at cost)}}$

Imagine inventory in a store being taken at three points, the beginning, the middle, and end of the year.

	Inventory at Cost (millions)	Retail (millions)
Beginning	$1.3	$2.0
Middle	1.1	1.65
End	1.075	1.75
Average inventory	1.158	1.8

Purchases during the year were $5.3 million at cost, net sales were $7.1 million.

Then, stockturn is either

$$7.1/1.8 = 3.9 \text{ times a year}$$

or

$$5.3/1.158 = 4.6 \text{ times a year}$$

Stockturn varies with the nature of the middleman's business. Thus a jeweler turns stock twice a year, electronic calculators turn four or five times a year, apparel turns eight or ten times a year, and fresh produce turns fifty times a year or it loses its adjective fresh and becomes merely produce.

RETAILING ARITHMETIC

Gross margin is the difference between what the reseller pays and the price he sets, as we have seen. However, before a reseller can draw up his income statement, both cost and price must be adjusted. For simplicity, let us deal only with retailers from now on.

Retailers use more than just invoice cost for an item. Typically they add the cost of transportation to the invoice cost, and they subtract cash discounts from it. Imagine that the billed cost of an item is $40.00, its selling price $55.00, in-bound freight $1.60, and cash discounts $2.50. Then the item's cost would be

$$\$40.00 + 1.60 - 2.50 = \$39.10,$$

and the gross margin 29 percent. These figures would typically be presented like this:

Retail price		$55.00	100%
Invoice cost	$40.00		
In-bound freight	1.60		
Cash discount	(2.50)		
Cost of goods sold		39.10	71
Gross margin		15.90	29

(To report the transactions of an entire period, say a year, cost of goods sold would have to be adjusted for changes in inventory as well, but this raises financial accounting questions that we are not concerned with.)

Revenue needs some slight adjustments too. Let us imagine that the retail buyer has bought one hundred scarves that she sells for $55. But four of them are returned for full credit, and the price of a fifth is reduced from $55 to $45 because the customer complains that it is damaged. The first four give rise to returns, the fifth to allowances, and the adjustments to sales look like this:

Sales rung up on cash register (100 × $55)		$5,500
Returned items (4 × 55)	$220	
Allowances ($55 − $45)	10	
Returns and allowances		230
Net sales		5,270

Of course, the buyer will try to sell the returned items again.

Still more adjustment is needed. Retailers are not always fortunate enough to sell all the stock they buy. What is not sold must be marked down and sold at a reduced price. Let us now imagine not that the retailer has bought 100 scarves and sold 100, but that she has bought 107 and sold 100. Of the 100 she sold four are returned, of which three are resold at full price and one is resold after being marked down to $40. On a fifth scarf, she grants an allowance of $10. The seven unsold items are marked down: two sell for $40 and the last five for $30. Now we can look at the figures for the entire purchase in Exhibit 4-1.

Now it is easy to see the problem the retailer faces. She wants to set her original price so that after returns and allowances (and other reductions) she earns the gross margin she wants. Earlier we used the simple rule

$$\frac{\text{Cost of goods sold}}{1 - \text{Desired gross margin}}$$

to reach a price. Now we see that this gives a gross price, the price "at the cash register." What the retailer is really interested in is net price, the price after returns and allowances.

Exhibit 4-1
The Results of the Scarf Purchase

Revenues			
Of 107 scarves bought			
-Sell 100 scarves @ $55		$5,500.00	
Of 4 scarves that are returned			
-resell 3 @ $55		165.00	
-markdown 1 to $40 and resell it		40.00	
Of 7 scarves that did not sell			
-mark them down to $40 and sell 2		80.00	
Of the 5 still left			
-mark them down again, to $30,			
and sell 5		150.00	
Gross sales (at the cash register)		$5,935.00	104%
Less			
Returns (4 scarves @ $55) =	$220.00		
Allowances ($10 granted on one scarf)	10.00	230.00	4
Net Sales		$5,705.00	100%
Cost of goods sold	Per Scarf		
Merchandise @ invoice	$ 40.00		
Cash discount	(2.50)		
In-bound freight	1.60		
	$ 39.10 × 107	4,183.70	73
Gross Margin		1,521.30	27%

To derive the basic formula we need, let us look at another typical departmental income statement, this time ignoring returns and allowances:

			Column A	Column B
Planned sales		$213,000	106.5%	100.0%
Retail reductions		13,000	6.5	6.1
(markdowns				
and shortages)				
Gross sales		200,000	100.0	93.9
Merchandise cost	$127,800		63.9	60.0
Workroom	5,600		2.8	2.6
Cash discounts	(2,400)		(1.2)	(1.1)
Total costs		131,000	65.5	61.5
Gross Margin		69,000	34.5	32.4

Retail reductions are discounts given to employees, shortages, mark-downs taken to sell off stock, stealing by customers, and stealing by employees (employees steal a lot more than customers). Workroom costs are for alterations.

This is an income statement after-the-fact, but a department manager can estimate what her department's costs will be and use the estimates in planning her merchandise selection and pricing.

Her problem is this: she plans to buy merchandise worth $127,800, and she expects markdowns to run 5.5 percent, shortages 1 percent, work-room costs 2.8 percent, and cash discounts 1.2 percent. How much planned sales does she need to yield a gross margin of 34.5 percent? Which means, by how much must she mark up the merchandise?

She starts with the figures in Column A, which are percentages based on gross sales. She needs to convert them to column B, where they become percentaged on planned sales.

If you think for a moment or two, you may work out the formula. It is

$$GM = IM(100 + RR) - RR - AC + CD \tag{1}$$

where

GM = gross margin earned after retail reductions, workroom costs and cash
     discounts
IM = initial markon
RR = retail reductions
AC = alteration costs
CD = cash discounts

Here, all the figures are percentages. The buyer has retail reductions (RR) of $5.5 + 1 = 6.5$ percent, workroom costs (WC) of 2.8, and cash discounts (CD) of 1.2. Hence

$$GM = IM(100 + RR) - RR - AC + CD$$
$$IM(100 + RR) = GM + RR + AC - CD \tag{2}$$

$$IM = \frac{GM + RR + AC - CD}{100 + RR} \tag{3}$$

$$= \frac{34.5 + 6.5 + 2.8 - 1.2}{100 + 6.5} = \frac{42.6}{106.5}$$

$$= 40$$

She must markup the merchandise 40 percent, that is, to a price that yields planned sales of $127,800/(1 - 0.4) = $213,000$. Equation (3) makes clear what is going on. The figures in the numerator are percentaged on gross sales and are found in column A. Dividing these by 100 + RR gives figures that are percentaged on planned sales, in column B.

The slight complications in all this arise because the buyer sets planned sales and hence must think in terms of column B, but the figures that she uses to plan and control her department and on which her bonus is based are percentaged on gross sales, as in column A.

HOW TO USE MARKETING ARITHMETIC

1. Make sure you understand your distributor's business, from his point of view. If you don't already know the standard figures—return on investment, gross margin, turnover, sales per square foot, sales per linear foot, and markdowns—you should learn.

2. Talk to your distributors. Marketers rely heavily on their distributors, and you need to stay in touch with them.

3. Above all, use your knowledge of distributor's business to better understand and manage your own.

NOTE

1. Such a policy may give other benefits than simplicity. See, for example, Roger Dickinson, "Markup in Department Store Management," *Journal of Marketing* (January 1967), 32–34.

Chapter 5

Averages and Marginals—What Marginal Analysis Says

It is embarrassing to have to include this chapter, because to a micro-economist, the material it deals with is so obvious. And it *is* obvious, just as it is obvious to a beginning student of harmony what is wrong with parallel fifths and parallel octaves; just as it is obvious to a beginning cook thickening a sauce why a boiling liquid must be added slowly to beaten egg yolks; just as it is obvious to a beginning writer why this sentence is wrong: "She is one of those women who is cursed with beauty."[1] That is, it is not so obvious at all, except to those in the know who typically no longer remember when or why the ideas were not so obvious.

Hence this chapter is necessary even though some feel that it is obvious and that the material would not tax the brain of a midge. At least the reader may be comforted to know that the material is crucial to using marginal analysis.

THE MARGINAL PRINCIPLE

The marginal principle teaches one to base the economic analysis of a decision solely on marginal costs and marginal revenues. If the marginal revenues of some course of action exceed the marginal costs, do it. If marginal revenues are less than marginal costs, don't.

In the simplest of situations, the one beloved of microeconomists, it says that the owner of a small business should increase production as long as the extra revenue that comes from increasing production exceeds the extra cost. We might imagine the owner testing each proposed addition: "If I sell one more unit, will the revenue I get exceed the extra cost of producing it?" A more charming way of putting the point is found in this excerpt from an economic classic:

When a boy picks blackberries for his own eating, the action of picking is probably itself pleasurable for a while; and for some time longer the pleasure of eating is more than enough to repay the trouble of picking. But after he has eaten a good deal, the desire for more diminishes; while the task of picking begins to cause weariness, which may indeed be a feeling of monotony rather than of fatigue. Equilibrium is reached when at last his eagerness to play and his disinclination for the work of picking counterbalance the desire for eating. The satisfaction which he can get from picking fruit has arrived at its maximum: for up to that time every fresh picking has added more to his pleasure than it has taken away; and after that time any further picking would take away from his pleasure more than it would add.[2]

This to a microeconomist is the marginal principle in action.

The marginal principle does not look to average costs and average prices. In fact, the principle says that it is wrong to work with average costs and average revenues if one wishes to maximize (short-run) profits, a big if, but not one that is normally questioned in the textbooks.

If all the world thought in marginal terms there would be no more to it. But the world does not think in marginal terms, at least most of the time. It thinks in averages.

The average cost of a car made in Japan is $2,000 less than an equivalent car made in Detroit.

What this sentence says differs from what most people think it says. In rough terms, it says that the total cost of making all Japanese cars divided by the number of Japanese cars made is $2,000 less than the cost of an American car, where cost is figured the same way. That is, it says something about averages. To most people, however, it says something else— that the cost of producing *another* Japanese car is $2,000 less than the cost of producing *another* American car. That is, most people think it says something about marginals.

The marginal principle at first glance seems bizarre. It directs one's attention to the fringes, not to the core. "Don't worry about what the plant is doing now, just concentrate on changes in output." Or, "don't worry about how many berries you've picked or how many you've eaten, just worry about the next berry."

But the marginal principle does make sense. Of course it makes micro-economic sense. But more important, it makes common sense, because most organizations make small decisions most of the time. Some firms, it is true, face big decisions from time to time. IBM spent one-quarter of a billion dollars in the 1960s to develop its Model 360 line of computers. Had the line failed, IBM might have failed with it. Electric utilities that chose in the late 1960s and early 1970s to construct nuclear power plants faced big decisions in the 1980s: should they continue construction at very high cost, or should they cancel and write off the partially finished plant? For some, the numbers involved are so large that a wrong decision might lead to bankruptcy. Aircraft manufacturers regularly face bet-the-company decisions, perhaps as often as every few years.[3]

But most companies never face decisions of this magnitude. In fact, most decisions over which so much deliberation is spent are embarrassingly slight—whether to buy this brand of word processor or that, raise prices by 3 or 5 percent, hire two or three new salesmen, hire a consultant, shade a price to close a deal, hedge a foreign exchange transaction, contest a grievance. These decisions are the small change of corporate life, and it is for them that the marginal principle makes economic and common sense. *Because* they are not big enough to affect any other part of the organization, one is safe merely comparing marginal costs and marginal revenues, secure in the knowledge that if the net of the two is positive, profits will increase.

• One example arises in politics. When a labor union (or a wealthy individual) buys a congressman by donating to his election campaign, just what is it the union is buying?[4] Many observers of the political scene say that what the union buys is access. It is a fine thing to exchange views with politicians, but with a little money they hear you better. How could it be that so slender a return is worth so much money? The reason is that most issues that come before Congress are of little importance. They are not great questions of state, they do not engage deeply held moral principles, they do not affect an important group of constituents. In our terms, they are marginal. As they are of little importance to the congressman and his reelection chances, he is open to persuasion, and perhaps reason. A fat donation merely provides the key to open the door allowing the contributor to tell his side of the story.[5]

• Consider supermarkets, where checkers take in coupons from customers. The store typically collects all the coupons for a week, sends them to a clearinghouse (usually in Mexico or Haiti) and after eight to ten weeks receives a check for the coupons. A typical coupon is worth thirty-six cents

Face value	$0.30
Handling fee	0.08
Gross amount due retailer	0.38
Clearinghouse fee	(0.02)
Cash flow to retailer from handling the coupon	0.36

Is it accurate to rely only on these marginal figures, or should we add in some overhead?

An average store receives some 110,000 coupons a year, or 2,100 a week. On a busy day like Friday, when it does one-quarter of its week's sales, the store probably gets one-quarter of its coupons, about 530, which spread over eight or ten registers gives some sixty coupons per register. Time and motion studies show that a checker can process a coupon in six or seven seconds.

So the time required to handle all 530 coupons that are presented on

Fridays is roughly an hour for all registers, or six or seven minutes per register over the entire day. Clearly handling coupons is a fringe activity, and in most analyses of coupon handling proposals, one will make the best decision by focusing solely on marginal values.

• Movie theaters show mostly movies and coming attractions. Paid advertisements in these theaters occupy only a few minutes in a show running a few hours, and require neither more equipment nor labor. The decision to run such advertisements can be correctly made using nothing but incremental analysis—how much extra revenue the ads will bring in versus how much extra it will cost to screen the ads.

This then is the premise on which the marginal principle rests—that the decision is so small that it has no effect on the rest of the organization. The decision can then be treated in isolation, as it were, with only the extra costs and extra revenues associated with the decision counted. There is no need to figure average costs, because they include costs that are unaffected by the decision.[6] Nor (the argument goes) is there any need to figure total costs and revenues.

With a few minor changes the marginal principle holds for medium-sized decisions involving (say) millions of dollars, or tens of millions. But for the most important decisions, those involving major commitments over long periods of time where there is substantial uncertainty about the future, the marginal principle is of little use. It is not that the marginal principle is wrong in such cases. It is not. It is that such decisions are no longer on the edge of the organization. They affect the entire organization, and they affect it in ways that are difficult to reduce to numbers. As a result, a marginal analysis for such decisions is rarely done, and when it is done it can not be believed.

How Microeconomists Teach the Marginal Principle

Faced with a decision, one asks two questions: Which alternative is best, and by how much? Surprising as it may seem, given the centrality of the marginal principle in microeconomics, the marginal principle deals with only the first. It deals, that is, with relatives, not absolutes. It selects the cheapest way to go from Boston to Dallas, but it does not even hint as to how much cheaper. The best alternative is best, that's all. Whether it is best by a penny or a million pennies does not enter the analysis.

This is a qualitative logic, then, not a quantitative one. It will surprise at least a few readers to learn that microeconomics, the most rigorous and mathematical of the social sciences, does not treat of numbers, but this is the case. The laws of economics, such as they are, contain no constants; and microeconomists spend most of their time working with economic models in which the important economic factors are represented by letters, partly because letters are more elegant and more abstract, but mostly because no one knows what numbers to use in place of the letters. Of course, in applying the theory, microeconomists must measure and compute, but most of the time measuring and computing stand in last place.

To answer the second question—how good is the best choice—the businessman uses totals or averages. He subtracts the total costs of a course of action from the total revenues, or (sometimes) he compares average costs with selling price, which in most cases is average revenue. (In fact, the businessman uses totals to answer both questions, which is best and by how much.)

The microeconomist answers the second question by comparing averages. But true to the innumerate nature of economics, the microeconomist uses the averages not to see by how much better the best alternative is, but rather to determine whether or not it produces a profit.[7]

How can it be that the world seems to get along without using the marginal principle all the time? By using totals. Were a cost analyst to evaluate plant operating costs at several levels of output, he would estimate for each the total labor needed, total materials, total power, and so on. Then he would total the totals, and use them in further analysis. He would not compute marginal costs from the totals, although it is easy to do. Suppose, for example the figures were

Output (in units)	80	90	110	120	135
Total plant costs ($)	600	700	900	990	1,185

As output increase by ten units, from eighty to ninety, total plant costs increase by $100, so the marginal cost is $100/10 or $10 a unit. In like fashion the other marginal costs are

Output (in units)	80	90	110	120	135
Total plant costs ($)	600	700	900	990	1,155
Marginal cost ($/unit)		10	10	9	11

But, to repeat, no one would ever do this to solve management problems. Real managers use totals.

Then why do microeconomists emphasize the marginal principle? Because it is so useful in studying microeconomics and because it is indispensable in making more microeconomics. Microeconomists prove theorems and try to predict (say) how markets will behave by using marginal analysis. Sometimes they imagine that managers use marginal analysis in making decisions, which managers usually do not. Sometimes they seem to recognize that managers do not use marginal analysis; but because this recognition strikes so deep at the core of microeconomic thinking, they do not wish to face the implications. This leads them to say something like this: We know that managers do not use marginal analysis but we pretend they behave *as if* they do use it. This murky two-word phrase allows the microeconomist the intellectual equivalent of having his cake and eating it. The microeconomist acknowledges the world as it is, and then simply ignores it all and goes about his business. (All this has been discussed in Chapter 2.)

The most vivid argument along these lines has been made by Milton Friedman. He asks us to imagine a billiards player whose shots we want to predict. We know the player is not a physicist, and we know that he does not solve a set of differential equations to figure out where to shoot and how. But we can analyze some of his behavior at the table *as if* he did these things. Oddly enough this seems to give Friedman confidence in the hypothesis that the billiards player is in fact a lightning calculator.

Our confidence is not based on the disbelief that billiard players, even expert ones, can or do go through [this process]; it derives rather from the belief that, unless in some way or other they were capable of reaching essentially the same result, they would not in fact be *expert* billiard players.[8]

The reader is invited to chew on "in some way or other."

AVERAGES

To some readers, perhaps most, this section on averages will be familiar. Feel free to skip on ahead.

To use marginal thinking, one must be able to estimate marginal quantities, and that means telling averages from marginals, average costs from marginal costs, and average revenues from marginal revenues.

Averages are easy to use and easy to understand, at least they seem easy. They do present four difficulties, nevertheless.

There Is More than One Average

The first problem with averages is that statisticians use not one but many averages: mean, median, mode, trimean, biweight, geometric mean, trimmed mean, Windsorized mean, and so on. The first three are all that most people ever encounter, however. As all three have their uses, one should try to develop some understanding of each. The mean of a set of values is the sum of the values divided by the number of values. The median is the middle value after all the values have been arranged in order. The mode is the value that occurs most often. Suppose we have five numbers, 9, 1, 1, 7, and 2. The mean is 4, the median 2, the mode 1.

The most familiar is the *mean,* often called the arithmetic mean. It lies at the heart of most statistical procedures. As a tool for describing data, it serves best when the values are compact and show a rough symmetry, in that they are roughly evenly distributed above and below the mean. The mean of 1, 50, and 99 is 50, but 50 does not describe the data well. Were the numbers 44, 48, and 58, the mean of 50 would be more typical and hence more informative to the user.

The desirability of an evenly spread distribution above and below the mean can be seen in the problem of describing the performance of a fullback who during a football game carries the ball fifteen times. One carry is a forty-two-yard dash, the other fourteen times combined total thirty-four yards. His overall average is 76/15 or 5.1 yards per carry, but his typical run is 34/14 or 2.4 yards. Here the sensible way to describe his performance is to caution the reader: either (1) his overall rushing average is 5.1 yards a carry, but he had one long run that inflated that considerably, or (2) his typical run is 2.4 yards, but in this particular game he had one long run and averaged 5.1 yards a carry. This example shows that when there are extremes, the mean may no longer describe the numbers well. Note, however, that these are problems not with the mean, but with people who use the mean.

The *median* also describes widely spread data poorly, but it offers some protection against asymmetry, outlying values, and distributions with long tails. But because it does not so much describe the data as the ranks of the data, it contains less of the information on the numbers than the mean does. This is its blemish; if the mean is a bowl of porridge, then the median is a bowl of gruel.

The *mode* is the fashionable value, the one that occurs most often. Pie a la mode is nothing more than pie served according to the fashion. For this reason, the mode can be seen as the typical representative of a distribution of values. When the spread of the data from low to high is large, the mode can represent the data better than either the mean or the median, because it indicates the largest subgroup in the data. Like the median it is little affected—pulled up or pulled down—by extremes, but also like the median it contains less information than the mean.

Averages Need Not Be Representative

The second problem with averages is that they do not necessarily represent any one object that they describe. Even today one may encounter a naïf who finds an impossible average amusing, for example the all-American family with its 2.2 children or the news story that reports that men buy only one-third of a pair of pajamas per year. On those rare occasions when one must deal with such refreshing simplicity, one need do no more than recast the statement: on average men buy one pair of pajamas every three years.

Averages Are Too Brief a Description

The third problem with averages has already been suggested—averages conceal the spread of values around the average. An average is just a single number. It is easy to forget the values from which the average was computed. For example, what does an average temperature of 65° F mean? "It means that we sweat six months of the year and freeze the other six, so on average it's just right." To make sense of average temperatures one must know how the temperature varies within the day and by season. That is, one must go behind the average and examine averages of parts of the whole.

• Exhibit 5-1 shows that the mean per capita consumption of sweeteners in the United States in 1980 was 134.3 pounds a year, or 2.6 pounds a week, and that the consumption of sugar alone was 83.2 pounds a year or 1.6 pounds a week. It also shows that most of the sweeteners were used not at home but in manufactured products—pastries, soft drinks, candy, ice cream, ketchup (which is some 20 percent sugar by weight), and even beer. A large proportion of the population, probably around half, will be below average in sweetener usage, and, of course, the rest will be above average, and some part, teenagers presumably, well above average. To

Exhibit 5-1
Per Capita Consumption of Sweeteners, 1980

		pounds	
A.	By Type of Sweetener		
	Sugar	83	62%
	High fructose syrup	19	14
	Glucose syrup	18	13
	Dextrose	4	3
	Saccharin	9	7
	Total Per Capita Consumption	134	100%
B.	By Use		
	Baking	18	13%
	Beverage	39	29
	Confections	14	10
	Dairy	7	5
	Food Processing	12	9
	Other	13	10
	Total Industrial Uses	103	77
	Non-industrial Uses	31	23
	Total Per Capita Consumption	134	100%

Source: Schnittker Associates, *Sweetener Markets and Policies—The 80's* (Washington, D.C.: Sugar Users Group, 1983), 9–10. Figures in A and B do not add because of rounding.

make sense of average consumption of sweeteners one must know how consumption varies within the population.

• In 1980 in the United States out of every one thousand live births 184 were illegitimate. Looking at subgroups behind this figure, one finds that the rate for whites was 110 and for non-whites 484. Looking again from a different angle at teenage girls age fifteen to nineteen, most of whom should still be in high school, the rate was 330 for whites and 821 for non-whites. The overall average of 184 does in fact tell us something; but the averages for the subgroups tell us a good deal more.[9]

• In 1984 the sales of the direct selling industry (by one estimate) were around $8.6 billion, sold by some 5.8 million door-to-door salesmen, now more grandly called independent sales contractors. The average sales per salesman is $8.6 billion/5.8 million = $1,500. But the turnover of such salesmen runs around 100 percent a year, and as with most sales forces, the few sell a lot, the many sell little. One figure commonly afloat among direct sellers is that 10 percent of the salesmen produce 80 percent of the sales.

Taking this figure at face value, we can guess at a (slightly) more detailed picture by halving the number of salesmen to (say) three million to take account of the 100-percent turnover. Then 10 percent sell 80 percent:

$$\frac{80\% \text{ of } \$8.6 \text{ billion}}{10\% \text{ of } 3 \text{ million}} = \$23,000$$

while the remaining 90 percent average

$$\frac{20\% \text{ of } \$8.6 \text{ billion}}{90\% \text{ of } 3 \text{ million}} = \$637$$

Since these are sales not commissions, we see immediately why the 90 percent quit, and we guess that many or most of the remaining 10 percent sell only part-time.

The moral is, compute averages for subgroups when it is possible. When it isn't, fake it, as in the direct selling example above, where the computations mix a few facts, some guessing, and a rule of thumb. When you can't even fake it, fall back on good habits of mind and clear thinking. Train yourself to recall the spread of values lying behind the average. "There's an average," one should say, "but I mustn't forget the values that lie behind it, spread out on both sides." This habit of mind will protect you—if you need protection—from being taken in by one-third of a pair of pajamas a year. It may help in more substantial ways, too.

• If you ask a group of consumers how many issues of a monthly magazine they read each year, you will find the average is somewhere in the middle, say four, six, or eight issues a year. But now stop to think.

Most magazine readers fall into one of two groups, loyal readers and infrequent readers. The overall average, right in the middle, mixes both and describes neither. In fact, the distribution of number of issues read is bowl-shaped, with many saying they read none at all or one or two issues; many saying they read ten, eleven, or twelve issues; and relatively few saying they read four, six, or eight. In this case, the best thing to do is not even to use the overall average, but to report two averages, one for readers and one for nonreaders.

• Fundraisers who use direct mail expect to get mostly small donations, say on the order of $20 or $30 or $40. But not all. Some donations run into hundreds of dollars. In such cases a single average is not a good overall summary. Instead most fundraisers report two averages, an overall average, and a second average excluding large gifts, say gifts over $100.

Spread: One Step Beyond the Average. Beyond an awareness of subgroups in the data and the fact that it spreads out on both sides of the average, one must look to another aspect of the data, how wide its spread is.[10]

The simplest measure of spread is the range, the largest value less the smallest. But it is not a good measure of spread because it depends so heavily on which largest and which smallest happen to show up in the sample, and as it is computed from only two numbers in the sample, it is just more informational gruel. More useful measures of spread are available, the most common being the standard deviation.[11]

Averages Can Be Knocked Off Course by Odd Values

The fourth problem with averages is a technical difficulty that occasionally causes problems: in small samples the mean can be markedly affected by errors, extreme values, and outliers. Thus the average of 11, 12, and 13 is 12. But if the 13 is erroneously entered as 31, a common typo, the mean jumps by 50 percent to 18.[12]

Marketers make frequent use of income distributions and average incomes, but such distributions are rarely symmetric: they are chopped off at the low end because incomes don't go below zero, but they can stretch out a long way on the high end because there are people who earn incomes many times larger than average. The mean of such a distribution, called a skewed distribution, is pulled toward the long tail and, particularly in a small sample, can mislead the unwary. In describing the average incomes of their readers, most reputable magazines avoid this difficulty by using the median income instead of the mean income.

This sensitivity to errors and extreme values is most serious in small samples. But one can find large differences between means and medians even in large samples, as the following figures on bank marketing expenditures show.

Average Bank Marketing Expenditures (in thousands) by Asset Size (in millions)

	Under $10	$10– 25	$25– 50	$50– 100	$100– 250	$250– 500	$500– 1,000	$1,000– 5,000	Over $5,000
Mean	$13	$17	$35	$56	$123	$244	$536	$1,421	$5,099
Median	8	13	29	55	115	226	450	1,163	3,551

Source: *Analysis of 1990 Bank Marketing Expenditures* (Chicago: Bank Marketing Association, 1990), 10 and 13. © 1990 Bank Marketing Association. Reprinted with permission. All rights reserved.

In all of the asset sizes, a few heavy spenders skew the distribution of expenditures and pull the mean above the median.

This section has discussed four problems with averages. There is one more. It is the folk errors and elementary errors of logic that one associates with journalists, political activists, chat show hosts, and politicians who reason like this:

The figures are shocking. I refer to the new study published by that great university in my great state which shows that half of America's school children, its new generation and its hope for the future in these dark and parlous days, is below average in health and even in these days of austerity and new recognitions and awarenesses that the federal government and the states can not be all things to all men—and women—and to children, too—it is also true, I say, I think that something should be done about this serious problem, and here is what I . . .

MARGINALS

An average is a total divided by a total. A marginal is a change divided by a change. They are not the same.

Average sales per salesmen is total sales for all salesmen divided by the number of salesmen. Marginal sales per salesman is the change in total sales when the number of salesmen is increased (or decreased) by one. Average sales per call is total sales divided by the total number of sales calls. Marginal sales per call is the change in total sales when the salesman makes one more call (or one less). Average cost per sales call is total costs of all sales calls divided by the total number of sales calls. Marginal sales per sales call is the increase in costs when a salesman makes one more call (or the decrease when he makes one less).

Why belabor such an obvious point? Because if one is to understand marginal analysis and use it, one must not only know that averages and marginals differ—one must be able to tell them apart.

I have been unable to locate any folk wisdom on averages and marginals; that is, folk sayings or maxims that might instruct one to avoid averages. The most important reason is, perhaps, that the world lives by averages. To most questions, only averages are given as answers. Ask a cost accountant what the cost of a sales call is and he will tell you—the average cost. Ask him what the cost of an extra sales call is, and he will tell you that he doesn't know, that the figures he has do not allow him to say.

Examples of the Confusion of Averages with Marginals

It is easy to confuse averages and marginals. One needs training and some practice to distinguish one from the other. Here are two standard examples.

• Many of the top graduate business schools do not offer night classes for students who work during the day. (They may have night classes for their regular full-time students, however.) But if you confine your analysis solely to money, the argument for offering night school courses is strong. Night school programs can be real money makers.

The argument is, of course, a marginal one. The school already has a library and an admissions office and catalogs and deans and elevators. It is heated in the winter and cooled in the summer whether or not there are night courses, because full-time students and faculty are in the building. None of these costs will increase. What extra costs there are are low— typically the night school needs a director, perhaps a secretary, and of course some faculty. Fortunately people who would like to do a little teaching can always be found, cheap; and by dropping courses that fail to enroll enough students to cover the instructor's salary it is easy to ensure that the program pays for itself. If instructors get (say) $5,000 a course and tuition is $700 a course, then unless the course enrolls at least eight students, it is canceled.

• The other standard example of the difference between averages and marginals is the income tax. Suppose one is considering whether to take on a four-week assignment that pays $10,000. No one would figure his after tax income using his average tax rate. He would compute using his marginal rate. If his marginal rate is 28 percent, the assignment is worth $7,200 in after tax income. Yet most people are unable to do this modest computation because they do not know the difference between marginal and average (and because they don't know their marginal rates and because they don't get many opportunities to earn an extra $10,000).[13]

The typical reader might think that this is nothing more than academic pettifoggery. But some feminists have found this issue freighted with Political Meaning. Here is how it works.

John works, but his wife Jane, a CPA, stays home to care for the children. John pays federal and state taxes, say, at a marginal rate of 38 percent and an average rate of 19 percent. Now Jane returns to work. To a microeconomist the analysis is straightforward. Because Jane's income is marginal, it must be considered in marginal terms, as must all her other incremental, job-related expenses—clothing for work, lunches, commuting, day care, perhaps cosmetics and extra beauty treatments, and perhaps work tools like a laptop computer or a calculator. (Note that all these are direct, avoidable costs.) When all these plus the taxes are added up, it turns out that Jane nets only 36 percent of her income, which turns out to be a measly $8 an hour.

To the microeconomist this all makes sense. Jane is *supposed* to compare the time and energy she puts into work and her lost leisure with the eight bucks an hour. How else can she decide whether she wants to work?

Here are typical figures for two different families:

	High Income, High-Tax Family				Low Income, Low-Tax Family			
	He Works, She Doesn't (000)		*Both Work (000)*		*He Works, She Doesn't (000)*		*Both Work (000)*	
Income		$70		$120		$25.0		$41.0
Taxable income		58		102		13.0		29.0
Taxes								
Federal	12		25.0		2.0		3.9	
State/local	6		12.0		.8		2.0	
Social security	4	22	8.0	45	1.9	4.7	3.1	9.0
Other expenses								
Day care			16.0				3.1	
Clothing			.6				.8	
Lunches, etc.			2.0				1.0	
Other			1.6	20				4.9
What they have left		48		55		20.3		27.1

Source: Based on Tamar Lewin, "For Some Two-Paycheck Families, the Economics Don't Add Up," *New York Times* (April 21, 1991), Sec. 4, 18.

Now politics enters: Should these incremental expenses be considered Jane's?[14] "It's unfair to say that child care or extra cosmetics must come out of the mother's salary," goes the argument. "It is a family expense, like the mortgage or the heat."

But day care is an avoidable expense—if one parent stays home.

Why is it the woman who stays home? The microeconomist has a straightforward answer. On average, women earn less than men, about one-third less. So the opportunity cost is lower for her to stay home. Feminists have a different answer.

MARGINALS AND AVERAGES ARE EASY TO CONFUSE

To repeat, it is easy to confuse marginals and averages. Let us look at some examples.

• In discussing the economics of the grocery trade, Fred Powledge writes that grocers make a gross margin of about 22 percent, which after deducting labor, interest, rent, heat, advertising, and the like leaves the grocer with a net profit on sales of around 1 percent.

When expenses are deducted, the store is left with a net profit of less than one cent on the dollar. That does not mean the typical supermarket makes less than one percent profit . . . it means that's the net profit on each item it sells, each time it sells it.[15]

Powledge makes two errors in his second sentence. First, the typical supermarket does in fact make a net profit of about 1 percent, which means that the profit and loss statement for a typical supermarket looks something like this:

Sales	100%
Less: cost of goods sold	78
Gross margin	22
Less: all other expenses, like labor,	
interest, rent, heat, advertising	21
Income before tax	1

Second, 1 percent describes the *average* profitability of the entire business, not the marginal profit made on any one sale. At the margin, an added dollar of sales generates twenty-two cents of extra cash. It makes no sense to say that extra sales of $100 increases profits by $1, although that might be something the supermarket might want to publicize and to stress in training its employees to be cost conscious. Once the supermarket is open for business, $100 more sales will increase profits by $22. The marginal value in this case is twenty-two times the average value.

• According to a story in the *Wall Street Journal,* the automotive industry makes up approximately 3 percent of the gross national product, but in the mid-1980s *changes* in auto output accounted for about 30 percent of quarterly *changes* in economic activity. The marginal importance of the automobile industry is about ten times higher than its average importance.

• Each year McGraw-Hill Research and *Sales & Marketing Management* report average sales call costs in the business press. The costs typically run on the order of $150 to $250 a call.[16] This figure is a total divided by a total—the total cost of all sales calls divided by the total number of sales calls. That is, it is an average. It does not say how much costs would increase if a salesman managed to make just one more sales call a week, nor does it say how much would be saved if he made one less. Yet many in business act as if the reported figures did indeed say just that.[17]

• The financial press reported that Sainsbury, the English supermarket chain, was opening its 262nd store, and that the opening would create 250 new jobs in the chain. At the end of the previous fiscal year Sainsbury had had 253 supermarkets and had employed 39,780.

Marginal number of employees = 250 for the new store

Average number of employees = 39780/253 = 157 per store

The figures are rough, to be sure, but the averages and marginals are quite far apart.

• Publishers of books and magazines have two types of costs, those incurred before printing and those incurred to print. Those incurred before printing are one-time costs like editing, composition, and preparation of plates. Publishers who put out reference books like dictionaries or encyclopedias will have to pay for the manuscript as well. Those incurred to print, mostly paper, ink, binding and press costs, vary directly with the size of the print run. If a publisher selects a print run of (say) ten thousand, then all of the costs can be totaled and an average cost per book figured. But this is not what it would cost to print another ten thousand books. That cost would be only the printing costs of the next ten thousand books, and these marginal costs are very much lower than the average costs.

The same story holds for publishers of records, tapes, cassettes, video cassettes, compact discs, and computer software. Once the record or software has reached the production stage, marginal costs are very low. In 1987 for example, Microsoft introduced an integrated software package called Microsoft Works. It carried a list price of $195 but its variable cost was $18.[18]

• A piece in a magazine for women in business complained that women earned more than one-third of all the Ph.D.'s in the country yet accounted for only one-quarter of the tenured faculty. This, she wrote, was evidence of a Nefarious Plot. The writer simply confused the marginal—one-third of the Ph.D.'s in the current year—and the average—one quarter of the total faculty, meaning what you get when you divide the number of women who hold tenure by the number of men and women who hold tenure. The only way—the *only* way—that the average can increase is for the marginal figure to be greater than the average.

• How does one make sense of this? An election poll shows that voters are unhappy with the quality of their schools, but they still vote down a bond issue that might improve them. The quality of the schools is an average, some kind of overall evaluation of the school system. The bond issue deals with marginals, how much extra taxes the voters will have to pay to service the bonds versus the extra quality the bonds will buy. The two are not the same. A voter can think the first and vote the second without being inconsistent.

• At one time the Franklin National Bank was the twentieth largest bank in the United States. In the years before it failed, the man who was to become its chief financial officer happily approved loans if their yields were "average plus 1 percent," that is, if the loan yielded at least one percentage point above the bank's average cost of money. But late in 1973, not long before the end, when Franklin's average cost of money was between 5 and 7 percent, its marginal cost of money was some two to four percentage points higher, that is, between 7 and 11 percent. Every loan approved at "average plus 1 percent" lost money.[19]

Why is it so hard to get marginal information? Because the figures are not routinely provided. Why? The answers are (1) tradition, (2) requirements of accounting and other professional standards bodies, and (3) and most important, no one is asking the right questions.

The moral for the marketer is straightforward: ask for marginal costs and you will get them. Just ask for costs and you will get them, but they will be average costs.

EXAMPLES OF MARGINAL THINKING

• The federal government has long provided aid to families with dependent children (AFDC). But many use marginal analysis to argue that AFDC has been too generous. Imagine a woman with three children working full time at the minimum wage in 1970. She would have earned $275 a month before Social Security and taxes, and less than $250 a month after. She also would have been eligible for at least some AFDC money, say, $80 a month. So by working full time, the woman takes home something less than $330 a month. But if she did not work at all she could have received $225 a month from AFDC (the median figure in 1970).

This was her choice: don't work and receive $225 a month or work and receive $330. Twenty-two eight-hour days of work were worth an extra $105, or 60 cents an hour. Working generates more income, but most would not see the extra $105 as worth it.

• Automotive salesmen try to trade their customers up from low-priced models with few options to higher-priced ones with more options. The basic pitch is a marginal one: Here is what you have to pay for the basic car. But for only a little bit more you get attractive extra features.

• Continental Airlines was reported as using marginal analysis in 1962.[20] Chris F. Whelan, vice-president in charge of economic planning, reasoned that the bulk of its scheduled flights had to return at least their fully allocated costs like depreciation, insurance, and overhead.

After the line's basic schedule was set, Whelan looked at fringe flights and decided them on a marginal basis.

If your revenues are going to be more than your out-of-pocket costs you should keep the flight on.

Thus, if the out-of-pocket expenses of a flight were $2,000, fully-allocated costs were $4,500, and the flight grossed $3,100, the decision would be made to run the flight. Continental would have $3,100 − 2,000 = $1,100 more in the till than it otherwise would have.

This illustrates how the marginal principle might be used. It would be irreproachable, except for two problems. The airline relied on fully allocated costs for most flights. Using fully allocated costs vitiates the marginal principle as microeconomists understand it, and leads to their professional Slough of Despond, "a non-optimal solution." In addition, one searches the economics literature in vain for further clear, simple examples. It is no accident that this particular example was published in 1963 and was still showing up in the economics literature twenty-five years later. There are almost no other examples published.

• Just after deregulation in 1978, Braniff Airways was granted sixty-seven new routes, but it had only forty-five days to get them started. Being in a hurry usually increases costs, but for at least some of the new routes, the extra costs were low, because the new routes were add-ons. Thus a flight that normally flew past Columbus, Ohio, on its way to Chicago now stopped at Columbus at little extra cost; likewise for the flight that used to terminate at Kennedy in New York City but now flew on to Albany.[21]

In both of these cases the added costs were low, hence the number of passengers needed to pay the added costs was also low.

• Different areas of the country suffer different rates of use of medical procedures. Dr. John Wennberg found, for example, that

in Vermont the probability that . . . children will undergo a tonsillectomy has ranged from 8 percent in one hospital market to nearly 70 percent in another. In Maine, by the time women reach seventy years of age in one hospital market the likelihood they have undergone a hysterectomy is 20 percent while in another market it is 70 percent.[22]

How could such sharp variations exist without affecting the health of the local population? It is probably because a large proportion of the care that doctors provide yields only a small net benefit; that is, the benefits and the risks are about in balance.

• Political fund raisers develop lists of people who respond to their appeals. As elections draw close, these fund raisers may return to the same list over and over, each time with a different appeal. As a list is used again and again, its yield begins to decline. But as long as the list yields more than the cost of the mailing, as long as the extra revenue exceeds the extra cost of the mailing, the marginal principle would dictate yet another mailing.

• Here is a more complex example of the confusion that can arise between averages and marginals. The traditional method of reducing cannibalization among chickens is to debeak them. But debeaking so deranges the hens that some 9 percent of them die before they can begin to lay. A new method of reducing cannibalization, developed in the mid-1970s, used contact lenses that distorted the hens' vision so they could not peck each other. The lenses cost more, but because fewer hens died, the farmers ended up with more eggs and more money.[23]

Let us first look at the standard profit and loss statements that would describe a year's output from a single hen.

Annual revenue from 22 dozen eggs @ $0.53 a dozen		$11.66
Annual costs		
Purchase of bird (adjusted for mortality)	$ 2.61	
Feed	7.04	
Labor	0.53	
Other costs and adjustments	(0.04)	
Cash costs plus labor	10.14	
Depreciation	0.26	
Interest	0.31	
Management	0.29	
Other costs	0.86	
Total cash and other costs		11.00
Annual profit per hen		0.66
Annual profit per dozen eggs ($0.66 / 22 dozen)		0.03

Let us assume a medium-sized chicken farm, one with 100,000 hens. Using contact lenses increases two costs: (1) the cost of the lens itself, which works out to $0.08 a bird, and (2) the cost of feed. The cost of the lenses will be 100,000 × $0.08 or $8,000. Feed costs go up for reasons that are of little interest to anyone but chicken farmers, but the increase is about $10,000. Using lenses on this farm, then, increases costs some $18,000, as follows:

Feed costs with contact lenses	$652,086	
Feed costs with debeaking	641,827	
Extra feed costs from using contact lenses		$10,259
Cost of the contact lenses		8,000
Total extra costs of using contact lenses		18,259

Now let us figure the extra profits from using contact lenses. Inserting contact lenses is easier on the hens than debeaking. As a result fewer die, 4.5 percent rather than 9 percent; and hens wearing contact lenses recover more quickly than debeaked hens, so they lay more eggs, on average one more egg a year. That is, of 100,000 hens, 4,500 will die after being fitted with contact lenses and 95,500 will survive to lay eggs; and of the 95,500, each will lay an average of two hundred and sixty-five eggs in a year, which is twenty-two dozen plus one. Of the 95,500 that survive, 91,000 would have survived anyway, after debeaking. So the new method yields an extra 95,500 − 91,000 = 4,500 surviving hens.

The standard profit and loss analysis is now clear.

4,500 more hens each laying 265 eggs a year	99,375 doz
91,000 hens each laying one more egg a year (91,000 × 1/12)	7,583 doz
Increase in annual egg production	106,958 doz
Times Average annual profit per dozen eggs per year	$ 0.03
Increase in annual profits before added costs	$ 3,209

Increased profits from extra eggs are $3,200, but the costs necessary to produce those extra eggs increase $18,000. The conclusion is clear: using contact lenses will reduce profits.

The conclusion is wrong.

This becomes clear when one does a marginal analysis, that is, when

Exhibit 5-2
Incremental Annual Costs and Annual Revenues of 4,500 Hens after Adopting the Contact Lenses

	Per Hen		
Extra annual revenues			
4,500 hens lay 22 dozen eggs @ $.53/dozen			
(4,500 × 22 × $.53)		$52,470	
91,000 hens each lay one extra egg			
(91,000 × 1/12 × $.53)		4,019	
Total extra annual revenues			$56,489
Extra costs	Per Hen		
Purchase	$2.61		
Labor	.53		
Fitting lenses	.08		
Other costs			
excluding feed	(.04)		
	$3.18 × 4,500 =	$14,310	
Extra feed		10,259	
Total extra annual costs			$24,569
Net of extra revenues and extra costs			$31,920

one looks only at things that change. The norm is 91,000 hens laying 22 dozen eggs a year. The figures in Exhibit 5-2 show that the contact lens will increase cash flow by some $32,000 a year.

Why the difference? The problem lies in the use of an average, namely the average profit of $0.03 a dozen. That figure already includes feed costs, so that when the *extra* feed costs are computed, the calculation gives a wrong answer.

Moral: there is nothing wrong with using averages. But they are tricky. Used without a good understanding of the procedures that underlie them, they can give wrong answers. Sometimes it makes sense to use marginals. But most of the time marketers should use totals.

IF MARGINAL ANALYSIS IS SO GREAT, WHY DOESN'T EVERYONE USE IT?

Because it's not so great. It is like a lot of other tools. When it fits the problem, use it; when it doesn't fit, don't use it. Everyone knows someone who knows one thing well and who uses that one thing when it makes sense and when it doesn't. Give a small boy a hammer and he will find a powerful lot of things that need hammering.

Marginal analysis fits when (1) you can get good estimates of the numbers, both the costs and the revenues, and (2) it is safe to confine the analysis to the numbers, that is, when other things are not more important. What other things? Other things like power, prestige, your own tastes and style, how will it play in the press, its effect on your career, what the corporation stands for, perhaps ethical concerns, and finally trade-offs between the short run and the long run. It is these other things, for example, that make most major graduate business schools sniff at night school programs, even though the money is easy.

The problem with using marginal analysis in marketing is that many important decisions arise in marketing where it is difficult or impossible to get numbers, or when other things dominate the decision. Take the important question of how much one should spend for advertising. This is not an issue where other things dominate, but it is one where it is often impossible to know what ad dollars will return. Hence the reliance on rules of thumb involving advertising-to-sales ratios or setting budgets at so much per case, per dozen, or per pound.

HOW TO USE MARGINAL THINKING IN ANALYZING MARKETING PROBLEMS

1. Make sure you understand the rationale of marginal analysis. It is not tricky, but it may violate what you think are sound principles of business.

2. Look for examples of marginal analysis in your reading and your daily life. You will be astounded at how often marginal thinking crops up.

3. Be wary of *averages*. Averages are enormously useful. But avoid automatically assuming that the average equals the marginal. Remember the supermarket, where the marginal value is twenty-times greater than the average value.

4. Don't expect a great deal from marginal analysis. There are so many areas of marketing where the idea is sound but it is too difficult to estimate extra costs and extra revenues.

5. Above all, remember that, like all microeconomics, marginal analysis is abstract. That means it leaves lots of important stuff out, like the strawberries for strawberry jam. So although it provides a sound basis for decision making, it is not enough.

NOTES

1. Parallel fifths and parallel octaves sound thin or harsh, and parallel octaves give too much prominence to the notes in the octaves, but beginning students usually lack the ear to hear these problems. You add the liquid slowly at first to avoid "shocking" the eggs and scrambling them, which would ruin the sauce. The second "is" should be "are." This becomes clear when the sentence is turned around: "Of those women who is cursed with beauty she is one."

2. Alfred Marshall, *Principles of Economics* (London: Macmillan, 1946), 331.

3. See for example John Newhouse, *The Sporty Game* (New York: Knopf, 1982).

4. Politicians come cheap; five or ten thousand is usually all it takes.

5. See Elizabeth Drew, *Politics and Money* (New York: Macmillan, 1983).

6. This will be qualified shortly. One needs average costs from time to time.

7. This oddity arises because microeconomists do not use numbers. When they solve their equations, they get a best solution, but they can not tell at first glance whether the best is the largest possible profit or the smallest possible loss. Hence the need for the additional step to work out whether or not the firm is running at a loss.

8. Milton Friedman, *Essays in Positive Economics* (Chicago: University of Chicago Press, 1953), 21.

9. Charles Murray, *Losing Ground* (New York: Basic Books, 1984), 262.

10. A pedant would note that "data" is plural (the singular is "datum") and write, "subgroups in the data and the fact that they spread out." I am a pedant, but not that kind of pedant.

11. If you want to know what this is, see your family statistician, or look into any elementary statistics book.

12. The source of this problem lies in how the mean is figured:

$$\frac{11 + 12 + 13}{3} = \frac{11}{3} + \frac{12}{3} + \frac{13}{3}$$
$$= 3.67 + 4 + 4.33$$
$$= 13$$

Here each term contributes about the same to the overall average. But with the typo we have

$$\frac{11 + 12 + 13}{3} = \frac{11}{3} + \frac{12}{3} + \frac{31}{3}$$
$$= 3.67 + 4 + 10.33$$
$$= 18$$

with the typo strongly influencing the result.

13. In one study of charitable giving, respondents were asked, "If you contributed another one hundred dollars to charity, how much would it save you in taxes?" Only one in five gave an answer that could conceivably be right, although the higher the respondent's income the more likely he was to give a possibly correct answer. See Commission on Private Philanthropy and Public Needs, *Research Papers Sponsored by the Commission on Private Philanthropy and Public Needs, History, Trends, and Current Magnitudes,* Vol. 1 (Washington, D.C.: Department of the Treasury, 1977), 177–178.

14. For a brief discussion of this question plus a look at non-sexist bookkeeping, see Caroline Bird, "The Truth About the Money She Earns," Chapter 7, *The Two-Paycheck Marriage* (New York: Rawson & Wade, 1979), 126–148.

15. Fred Powledge, *The Fat of the Land* (New York: Simon & Schuster, 1984), 131.

16. For example, see the 1990 "Survey of Selling Costs" reported in *Sales & Marketing Management.*

17. The quality of information collected in these surveys is strained. For example, McGraw-Hill Research surveys sales managers by mail and lets them decide for themselves which personnel costs to include and which to exclude. Inevitably each respondent chooses differently, and the comparability of the resulting responses goes out the window.

18. Thomas V. Bonoma and Thomas J. Kosnik, *Management Management* (Homewood, Ill.: R. D. Irwin, 1990), 570 (part of a case study).

19. Sanford Rose, "What Really Went Wrong at Franklin National," *Fortune* (October 1974), 120.

20. *Business Week* (April 20, 1965), 111, 112, 114.

21. John J. Nance, *Splash of Colors* (New York: William Morrow & Co., 1984), 122.

22. John E. Wennberg, "Dealing with Medical Practice Variations: a proposal for action," *Health Affairs* (Summer 1984), 49.

23. The figures come from "Optical Distortion," a Harvard Business School case.

Chapter 6

The Marketing Control Statement

The marketing control statement is an example of how marginal analysis is used in marketing.

The marketing manager needs a separate set of books on his operations. The reason is that standard cost control and accounting systems were designed not for marketing but for manufacturing operations. Indeed, cost accounting was developed to serve the needs of factories, long before marketing reached importance as a business function.

Financial accounting, after all, aims to meet certain legal reporting requirements and to provide the public (including lenders and the government) with information. Just as accounting procedures are designed with these ends in mind, one can design accounting procedures with marketing decisions in mind.

Fortunately, the process involved is relatively simple and therefore relatively inexpensive. The result gives the marketing manager a much clearer view of the financial implications of his decisions.

HOW TO PREPARE A MARKETING CONTROL STATEMENT

To see what a marketing control statement is and how to construct one, let us work with an example. Here is the income statement for an industrial product selling thirty-five thousand tons a year worth $100 million.

		(millions)
Sales		$100.0
Production		
Materials	$26.0	
Wages	15.0	
Variable-overhead	3.0	
Fixed-overhead	16.5	60.5
Operating income		39.5
Administration		
Sales force	$16.0	

Advertising	1.5	
Trade shows	0.4	
General and administrative	9.0	$ 26.9
Net income		$ 12.6

This income statement is a fair summary of the product's overall performance. But it is not particularly useful for marketing management, and it does not provide marginal figures. Let us see how to construct the more useful marketing control statement (MCS). Here are the steps:

1. Get variable production costs.

2. Get all other variable costs (for example, sales commissions, royalties, or sales discounts).

3. Get programmed marketing costs, those associated with the marketing program you are interested in.

4. Ignore all other costs, like general and administrative costs, and overhead. Do not put *any* allocated costs on the marketing control statement.

5. Fill out the blanks in the following table:

Pro Forma Marketing Control Statement

	Totals	Per Unit
Revenue	$ ☐	$ ☐
Less: variable costs	☐	☐
Gross marketing contribution	☐	☐
Less: programmed marketing costs	☐	
Net marketing contribution	☐	

In the example given above, the marketing control statement will look like this:

		Totals (millions)		Per Ton
Sales		$100.0		$2,857
Production costs				
Materials	$26.0		$743	
Wages	15.0		429	
Overheads—variable	3.0	44.0	86	1,257
Gross marketing contribution		56.0		1,600
Programmed marketing expenses				
Sales force	$16.0			

Advertising	1.5	
Trade shows	0.4	17.9
Net marketing contribution		38.1

The MCS lets you see where the money comes from. The gross marketing contribution (GMC) is the cash flow after the product has paid for its own manufacture. The net marketing contribution (NMC) is the cash after the product has paid for its own manufacture and marketing.

The method is simple, then. Sort all costs into three piles—variable, programmed, and all other; get sales; and put together the marketing control statement.

Most often the marketing control statement is prepared for a brand. But it can and should be prepared for anything that merits special attention—a brand, a product, a product line, a department, a promotional campaign, a profit center, a sales territory, an important customer, a country.

ADVANTAGES OF THE MARKETING CONTROL STATEMENT

1. The MCS shows the financial performance of the program *at the margin*. The MCS does not include *any* overhead or *any* allocated costs. This is the same as saying that it does not include any fixed costs. Thus, the MCS embodies the marginal principle. From the point of view of microeconomists, the MCS is how figures should be prepared.

Recall that marginal analysis applies to activities on the fringe of the business, in the sense that changes on the fringe don't change anything else in the business. (This is why the MCS excludes fixed costs. They don't change, so leave them out.)

Let us suppose that we manage to increase our net marketing contribution by $5 million, from $38.5 million to (say) $43.5 million. Since no other costs in the business have changed, all of the increase of $5 million will flow right to the bottom line, to the business's net income. That is worth saying again:

changes in net marketing contribution flow straight to net income, and from there to earnings per share.

2. Because the MCS contains no allocated costs, the only items on the MCS are cash flows. Thus, it is a "clean" statement—no costs based on tricky accounting conventions, no funny money. This means, for example, that if the product were to be sold to another firm, the figures on the marketing control statement, principally the net marketing contribution, would be the basis for negotiation on the value of the product.

3. Because it contains no allocations, the MCS is the tool to use to

compare yourself with your competition. You can't look over your competitor's shoulders to see their profit figures because you don't know how they allocate overhead and G&A to their products. But you should be able to make some good guesses as to their variable costs and most of their programmed costs.

This means you should be able to compare your MCS with theirs and thus get some insight into their operations.

4. The information on the MCS makes it easy to ask what-if questions. A change in price or variable cost will directly affect the gross marketing contribution, and hence the net marketing contribution. A change in programmed costs will affect only the net marketing contribution.

5. The per unit costs are essential in exploring break-even points and just-cover points, which we cover in Chapter 7. The format also makes it easy to explore such questions as, What will happen if my sales fall 3 percent and I temporarily cut back on my sales promotions or award some extra sales force incentives?

6. Dividing gross marketing contribution by share of market gives a rough indication of the value of a share point. There is a critical assumption here, however, namely that variable costs are roughly constant for small changes in market share. As this is probably true for most business most of the time, it is safe to calculate the value of a share point to your company.

One uses the value of a share point for quick break-even analyses. Suppose a share point is worth (say) $800,000 a year, and that the marketing manager is considering increasing his promotional spending by $2,400,000 in the coming year. The manager can quickly see that he needs roughly $2,400,000/$800,000 = 3 more share points to just cover the extra expenditure.

7. The MCS statement is easily adapted to a variety of circumstances. Suppose, for example, we are not interested in a single product, but in three products, all managed by the same product manager. The MCS must not contain allocated costs or it will lose its clean statement of cash flows. How should the product costs be handled? Like this:

	Product A	Product B	Product C	Product Line Totals
Individual Products				
Revenue	$1,000	$1,300	$1,900	$4,200
Variable costs				
Materials	260	400	640	1,300
Labor	150	135	290	575
Variable overheads	30	___	70	100
Total variable cost	440	535	1,000	1,975
Product GMCs	560	765	900	2,225

Programmed Product Costs

Sales force	$ 160	$ 140	$ 240	$ 540
Product advertising	45	40	100	185
Total programmed costs	205	180	340	725
Product NMCs	355	585	560	1,500

Programmed Line Costs

Product line management	$ 130
Product development	40
Line advertising	150
Total line costs	320
Total Line NMC	1,180

The MCS can also be extended to give a kind of return on investment. You have three sales territories, let us say, each with its own NMC. But each also involves investment in accounts receivable, finished goods, inventory, and some modest office equipment. Divide the NMC for each sales territory by its investment, and you get what has been called ROAM, return on assets managed.[1]

Marketing Control Statement for Three Sales Territories

	A	B	C
Sales	$1,300	$2,700	$550
Variable costs	589	1,224	249
GMC	711	1,476	301
Programmed costs	104	186	117
NMC	607	1,290	184

Here we see three territories with different levels of net marketing contribution. How can we compare them? One obvious answer is to compare actual results with planned results. It also makes sense to compare results with the assets used in the three territories.

Investments in the Three Sales Territories

	A	B	C
Accounts receivable	$ 355	$ 494	$ 369
Inventory	2,815	5,724	1,173
Office equipment	29	39	31
Total assets	3,199	6,257	1,573
Return on assets managed	19%	21%	12%

Territory A requires an investment of $3,199 and generates an NMC of $607. Hence, its ROAM is $607/3,199 = 19 percent.

Now we can see that territory C not only generates the smallest gross marketing contribution but is also returning the lowest ROAM. That means it is not getting as much NMC from its assets as the other two territories.

Some managers prefer to think of a return on investment as the product of two ratios, contribution to sales and sales to investment. The first shows what proportion of sales ends up as net marketing contribution; the second shows what level of sales the investment supports. Then,

$$\frac{\text{Net marketing contribution}}{\text{Sales}} \times \frac{\text{Sales}}{\text{Assets managed}} = \text{ROAM}$$

Here are the figures for the example just given:

An Alternative ROAM Calculation for Three Sales Territories

		A	B	C
Contribution/Sales	*a*	0.467	0.478	0.334
Sales/Investment	*b*	0.406	0.432	0.350
ROAM = *a* × *b*		0.190	0.206	0.117

That is, for territory A,

$$\frac{\text{NMC}}{\text{Sales}} = \frac{607}{1,300} = 0.467$$

$$\frac{\text{Sales}}{\text{Assets Managed}} = \frac{1,300}{3,199} = 0.406$$

and

$$\text{ROAM} = 0.467 \times 0.406 = 0.19 \text{ (or 19 percent)}.$$

A similar approach has been proposed for calculating a return on assets devoted to specific customers. In this approach, the net marketing contribution generated by a customer is divided by the sum of that customer's accounts receivable and the finished goods inventory devoted to his business. The result is a return on customer assets.[2]

The marketing control statement is little more than an empty rack, by means of which the marketing manager can organize his financial analysis. The basic idea is to sort all costs into three classes—variable, programmed, and all others—then ignore all the other costs to generate something very close to a cash flow statement for the marketing program being analyzed. It should be used on all programs whose size makes them worth management attention.

WHAT'S WRONG WITH THE MARKETING CONTROL STATEMENT?

The MCS does not serve all purposes, and there are arguments against it on other grounds as well.

The two principal arguments against the MCS and other systems like it are that (1) variable costs lead to prices that are lower than they can be and (2) variable costs alone provide poor information for decisions with a long-time horizon.

As for the first, variable costs are in fact a poor basis for setting prices, but then so are most other costs. The key influences on prices are, or should be, market demand and what competitors are asking. Then after a tentative price is set—without any attention being given to costs—the implications of the price for gross marketing contribution can be worked out using the MCS. The fault, that is, lies not with the variable costs but with the way prices are determined.

As for the second, there is a measure of truth in it too. The MCS is best for short-run decisions in which changes in fixed costs can be safely ignored. Once one begins to consider bigger decisions, like dropping a product line or setting up company-owned retail stores, the MCS no longer serves well.

But in such situations, full costs, the natural alternative where variable cost systems are not used, do not serve well either. Recall that what we are after is marginal (or incremental) costs. The argument made by full cost advocates is that full cost provides an estimate of *long-run* incremental cost, which is what you want in considering long-run decisions.

There are two problems with this view. The first problem is that full cost does not measure incremental cost, because over the long run, fixed costs change not only in total but in their makeup. That is, both the total *and* the structure of fixed costs change in the long run. Full cost does not reflect this well. The other problem arises from cost indivisibility. Certain costs must be incurred in large indivisible units. Committed to introducing a new product on a nationwide basis, a firm must spend what it takes. It is not possible to introduce nationwide on half a national budget. Indivisibilities lead to lower average costs as usage rates increase, but incremental costs will be lower still. Once again, full cost is misleading when judging long-run incremental cost.

There may be other (minor) problems as well. Sometimes top management does not like contribution accounting because it wants to keep variable cost figures to itself. Others feel that costs should provide at least rough estimates of competitive costs, which the MCS will not do.

Note, finally, that the MCS takes the short view. It exemplifies what some feel is wrong with American business—it focuses on the short run, on the quick fix, and makes it harder to take the longer view of what is best for the business over time.

WHAT'S WRONG WITH USING ALLOCATED COSTS?

There is nothing wrong with allocating costs, at least until something better comes along. The common objections to cost allocations do have some merit nevertheless.

1. To allocate costs one must choose a basis for the allocation. This choice usually turns out to be rough and ready, even arbitrary—for example, cubic feet in the warehouse, square feet in the plant, sales dollars for sales support expenses, and direct labor or machine hours or material quantities for product costs. But arbitrary does not mean capricious. And much of the corporate world, perhaps most of it, is comfortable using allocations.

2. Because there is no fundamental logic for preferring one basis for allocation over another, too much of management's time is spent resolving disputes as to which costs which department should bear.

3. Allocated costs violate the common sense of control that managers should be held responsible for the resources they use and for their expenses. Because allocations are inherently arbitrary, allocated costs do a poor job of measuring resources used.

4. Traditional cost accounting systems that rely heavily on allocated costs are decidedly inadequate for product costing and the analysis of profitability.[3] Perhaps the most frequent criticism of standard cost accounting practices points to cost distortion brought about by improper allocation of overhead costs. Critics often cite as one instance of cost distortions, systems that identify low-volume products as the most profitable and high-volume products as the least profitable.[4]

The reason is straightforward. The basis on which cost allocations are made is not even across all products. Take, for example, a product that is sold by the sales force to a variety of industrial buyers under a house brand, and that is also packed as private labels under long-term contracts negotiated by the president of the company. Sales of the house brand use a lot of sales force resources; private label sales use none. But a typical allocation of sales force expenses based (say) on sales dollars or gross margin will not serve either form of sales well.

In general, using standard allocation bases distorts the allocation of costs that vary by type of customer, type of distribution channel, number of product variants produced, even the number of batches of products made.

There are three morals.

1. Avoid allocations if you can.
   - The marketing control statement is an example.
2. Stay alert for signs that the cost accounting system is not giving you what you need. For example,
   - Products where the company has a natural advantage appear to have costs that are too high and hence low profits.
   - Special orders are just as profitable as normal orders.
   - Small accounts are just as profitable (as a percentage of sales) as large accounts.
   - Small volume items generate as much GMC (as a percentage of sales) as large volume items.
   - The company wins bids mostly for business that it doesn't want (for example bids for low-volume production items where the plant is best equipped to handle high-volume production).
3. Learn about activity-based costing. This is the current best bet to replace the traditional cost accounting procedures.[5]

HOW TO USE THE MARKETING CONTROL STATEMENT

1. Understand the basic idea behind the marketing control statement. Based on cash. No allocations. Couldn't be simpler.

2. Show that you understand contribution by never saying "profit" when you mean "contribution." Contribution is not profit. It is a contribution toward other expenses.

3. Run up marketing control statements on every piece of your business—every important brand, every important customer, every important division, every important sales territory, every important segment, and every important salesman.

4. Try to estimate your competitors' marketing control statements.

5. Recognize that the marketing control statement is an approach that can be modified to suit your needs.

NOTES

1. J. S. Schiff and Michael Schiff, "New Sales Management Tool: ROAM," *Harvard Business Review,* Vol. 45 (July-August 1967), 59–66.

2. Randy Myer, "Suppliers—Manage Your Customers," *Harvard Business Review,* Vol. 67 (November-December 1989), 162.

3. For a decidedly different view of cost accounting read what the Japanese do in Ford S. Worthy, "Japan's Smart Secret Weapon," *Fortune* (August 12, 1991), 72–75.

4. Robin Cooper and Robert Kaplan, "How Cost Accounting Systematically Distorts Product Costs," in *Accounting & Management: Field Study Perspectives,* edited by W. J. Bruns, Jr., and Robert S. Kaplan (Boston: Harvard University Press, 1987), 204–228.

5. To get started, see James B. Ayers, "Understanding Your Cost Drivers— The Key to Disciplined Planning," *Cost Management* (Fall 1988), 6–15; H. Thomas Johnson and Robert S. Kaplan, *Relevance Lost: The Rise and Fall of Management Accounting* (Boston: Harvard Business School Press, 1987); James A. Brimson, *Activity Accounting* (New York: Wiley, 1991).

Chapter 7

Break-Even Points and Just-Cover Points

Marketers find break-even analysis surprisingly useful; surprising because it is so simple an idea that it should have been bettered a long, long time ago. It is best to think of break-even analysis as one thinks of any other time-tested, trusty tool, like a thermometer or a jack knife, say— portable, cheap, easy to use, easy to understand, versatile—but by no means suitable for every job, and likely to break if applied to the wrong job or used in the wrong way.

THE TRADITIONAL VIEW OF A BREAK-EVEN POINT

As it is customarily used, the break-even point is that level of sales where total revenue equals total expenses, that is, it is the level of sales that makes the two sides of this equation equal:

$$\text{Total revenue} = \text{Net income}$$

$$\text{Sales} - \text{Variable expenses} - \text{Fixed expenses} = \text{Net income}$$

$$\text{Unit price} \times \text{Units} - \frac{\text{Unit variable}}{\text{expense}} \times \text{Units} - \text{Fixed expenses} = \text{Net income}$$

Managers who use break-even analysis typically apply it to an entire business. Thus, hoteliers say that they need to sell 65 percent of their rooms to break even. Or we read that "by dint of hard effort Ford has succeeded in reducing its breakeven point to 1.7 million cars a year," meaning that if Ford sells 1.7 million cars, it will just cover its fixed costs, with nothing left over for profit.

HOW MARKETERS USE BREAK-EVEN POINTS

Marketers do not use break-even analysis this way. They use it in three other ways: first, as a rough way of estimating a point on the demand schedule, which links volume with prices; second, as a way of studying the implications of a proposed course of action, of answering what if questions; third, as a quick and dirty way of assessing the risk of a proposal.

None of these have anything to do with breaking even in the usual sense of the word, because none apply to the business as a whole. Rather, they deal more with just covering a proposed expense. As a result, one might call them not break-even points (BEPs) but just-cover points (JCPs).

Marketers find it much more useful to think of BEPs or JCPs in terms of covering programmed costs. Then, the just-cover point is that level of sales that will just cover the programmed costs associated with the brand (or program).

Example: A software firm is considering a three-day seminar for users of its scientific word processing package. Variable costs—meals, coffee, and handouts—for the seminar will be around $40 per participant. The programmed costs of the program—renting the room, direct mail advertising, security, and the like—will run $6,000. These do not depend on the number of participants, of course. The participants will be asked to pay $240 each.

The First Use: Guessing Demand

We can calculate the unit gross marketing contribution (GMC):

Unit revenue per participant	$ 240
Variable cost per participant	40
Unit GMC	200

The marketing control statement (MCS) would be simple to draw up if the number of participants were known. But we won't know that number until we get responses to the mailing. Although the number of participants is not known, we can ask how many must attend the seminar to cover, just, the costs of the seminar.[1] The answer, as most readers surely know, is $6,000/$200 = 30 participants.

Now the guessing game begins. How likely is it that we will get thirty participants, given the price, the program, the advertising, and the site? No one knows, really, but managers can make rough estimates and guesses based on experience, and perhaps on hope. This is what, much of the time, serves marketers in lieu of estimates of demand. It is a poor substitute, but it is hard to do much better.

The Second Use: "What if" Questions

One can go further and ask, How many participants does the seminar need if it is to pay its costs and in addition, earn two thousand dollars in net marketing contribution (NMC)? Now the amount to be covered is

$6,000 in programmed costs plus $2,000 more in NMC. So the number of participants needed is

$$\frac{\$6,000 + \$2,000}{200} = 40$$

Now we can use this to deal with some what if questions. *What if* the fee is raised to $300? Then the unit GMC is 300 − 40 = $260, and to just cover $8,000 we need 8,000/260 = 31 participants. *What if* we raise the price to $250 and cut the programmed marketing expenses by $1,000 to $7,000 (including the entire NMC of $2,000). Then the unit GMC is $210 and the just-cover point is 34.

The Third Use: Rough Assessment of Risk

A break-even point implies a time to reach break even. The shorter the time, the lower the risk. If the break-even point is 300,000 units and you expect to sell 150,000 units a year, you expect to break even in two years. The payback period is two years. This payback period is a crude measure of risk because the quicker the payback, the less the risk. Or we might expect cash inflows and outflows to look like this:

	Cash		
Quarter	Outflows	Inflows	Cumulative
1	$40		$ (40)
2	65	$ 3	(102)
3	55	12	(145)
4	25	23	(147)
5	15	39	(123)
6	10	45	(88)
7	10	70	(28)
8	10	90	52
9	10	90	132

The cash in just offsets the cash out, sometimes in the seventh quarter.

Some books recommend interpolating to get a finer estimate of just when payback is reached in the seventh quarter. With the figures given here, by the seventh quarter cash is flowing in at the rate of 90 − 10 = $80 per 90 days or $0.89/day. So payback is reached 28/0.89 = 31.5 days into the seventh quarter, that is in about 7.3 quarters.

How Accurate Is Marketing?

I doubt whether it ever makes sense for a marketer to seek such refinement. Instead of saying the product above will break even in 7.3 quarters, the only honest thing to say is that the product will break even some-where around the seventh quarter.

This is inaccurate perhaps, but in predicting how customers respond, marketers must be satisfied with inaccurate figures. Accuracy is mea-sured in terms of significant digits. Think for the moment of a common occurrence: You see someone, a woman (say), and you ask yourself, how old she is. If you can get the right decade, your estimate is good to one significant digit; if you come within one year, it is good to two significant digits; and within one month, to three significant digits. Thus, to one significant digit: she's thirtyish; to two significant digits: she's thirty-six or thirty-seven; to three significant digits: she's thirty-seven and her next birthday is in March or April. My guess is that most people can get the right decade but few can come within a year or two; that is, most people can estimate age to only one significant digit.

Because its estimates build on guesses about what customers will do and what competition will do, marketing is a one-digit art. Perhaps I should say that marketing is at best a one-digit art.

Some Examples. Let us now look at some examples to better under-stand the method.

1. Company Channels of Distribution—Sometimes industrial mar-keters must choose between selling direct to end users or selling through original equipment manufacturers. OEM sales sell at a lower price than direct sales, but the programmed marketing costs—typically for selling, trade shows, advertising, and technical service—are lower as well.

Imagine a computer-aided design/computer-aided manufacturing (CAD/CAM) system that carries a variable cost of $5,250. A comparison of the two channels of distribution might look like this:

	Sell to OEMs	Sell Direct to End Users
Price	$13,100	$19,000
Variable cost	5,250	5,250
Gross marketing contribution	$ 7,850	$13,750
Programmed marketing costs	$1,194,000	$6,016,000
Number needed to just cover programmed costs	152	438

2. Blank Video Cassette Tapes—A company is considering selling blank video cassettes under its own brand name. The variable cost to purchase, load, pack, and inspect the cassettes runs $1.11, let us say. The introductory marketing plan will involve first year programmed costs of $6.74 million and a factory price of $3.27. The unit GMC is $3.27 − $1.11 = $2.16, and the number of cassettes that must be sold to just cover these first year costs is simply $6.74 million$/(3.27 − 1.11) = 3.1$ million units. If

the size of the market is 56 million cassettes a year, this implies a share of market of 3.1/56 or 5.5 percent.

3. Cannibalization by a New Product—A doughnut franchise wants to add a line of low sugar muffins, but it is worried that the muffins will hurt doughnut sales. A one-week test in two stores reveals the following:

	Gain from Muffins	Loss from Doughnuts	Difference
Estimated sales/store	$768	$320	$448
Variable costs @ 68%	522	218	305
GMC @ 32%	246	102	143

So in a year, muffins are likely to add around $143 × 52 = $7,500 extra GMC. Since a new oven costs just over $8,000, the payback period is a bit over a year, and a more careful analysis using discounted cash flow techniques is not necessary.

4. Southwest Airlines—In its early days, Southwest Airlines had flight expenses that ran on the order of $800 a flight. These were avoidable because Southwest incurred them if it flew the flight and avoided them if it didn't. Variable costs per passenger were low, about $3.

Now it is a simple matter to figure how many passengers are needed at several proposed fares to just cover the cost of a flight.

Proposed Fares	GMC per Passenger	Number of Passengers to Just Cover $800
$10	$ 7	115
20	17	47
26	23	35

SHORTCUTS TO FIGURING BREAK-EVEN AND JUST-COVER POINTS

There are five formulas for doing calculations like these. They can speed up the process—if you remember the formulas, and they are useful to put into your spreadsheet.

The question is the one we raised above. If we decrease the unit gross marketing contribution, how much must we increase unit sales to leave us just as well off? (Or if we increase the unit GMC how much can unit sales fall and still leave us just as well off?) The answer is

Formula 1

$$\frac{\text{Current unit GMC} - \text{Proposed unit GMC}}{\text{Proposed unit GMC}}$$

See the appendix for a derivation of formula 1.

Let us return to the Southwest Airlines (SWA) example. Suppose for a moment that the fare was $10 and that SWA was considering raising it to $20, then the formula gives

$$\frac{\$7 - 17}{17} = -\frac{10}{17} = -0.59 \text{ or } -59\%$$

The number of passengers can fall 59 percent and still leave SWA as well off as before. Since the just-cover point at $10 is 115 passengers, the just-cover point at $20 is 115 less 59 percent or 47 passengers.

Or we might suppose that the current fare were $26 and that SWA was considering a reduction to $20. Now the formula gives

$$\frac{23 - 17}{17} = \frac{6}{17} = 0.35 \text{ or } 35\%$$

Hence, the number of passengers must increase by 35 percent

$$35 + 35\% \text{ of } 35 =$$

$$35 + \quad 12 \quad = 47 \text{ passengers}$$

or SWA will lose contribution.

Changes in Gross Marketing Contribution

These simple examples illustrate the basic idea—to obtain a just-cover point, divide programmed costs (or fixed costs) by a unit gross marketing contribution. When the issue involves changing the unit GMC—when we change prices or variable costs—things get a bit more complicated, but only a bit.

Because marketers consider changes in the unit gross marketing contribution so often—because they are tinkering either with prices or with costs—it is handy to have formulas for just such situations. Let us look at an example to see how it is done.

Suppose we currently sell 60,000 cases a month at $10 a case. The variable cost is $6 a case, so our current MCS is as follows:

	Now (000)
Number of cases	60
Revenue	$600
Variable cost	$360
GMC	$240
Programmed marketing	$ 48
NMC	$192
Price per case	$10.00
Cost per case	$ 6.00

We think we can raise the price about 8 percent, from $10.00 to $10.80, but we expect to lose some of our case volume. How much can we afford to lose and still be no worse off? How many cases at $10.80 a case are needed to give us this just-cover MCS?

	Now (000)	Just Cover (000)
Number of cases	60	
Revenue	$600	
Variable cost	$360	
GMC	$240	$240
Programmed marketing	$ 48	$ 48
NMC	$192	$192
Price per case	$10.00	$10.80
Cost per case	$ 6.00	$ 6.00

It is a problem in high school algebra. But we can see what to do by making a simple substitution in the just-cover MCS.

	Now (000)	Just Cover (000)	(000)
Number of cases	60		NofCases
Revenue	$600		10.80 NofCases
Variable cost	$360		− 6.00 NofCases
GMC	$240	$240	4.80 NofCases
Programmed marketing	$ 48	$ 48	
NMC	$192	$192	
Price per case	$10.00	$10.80	
Cost per case	$ 6.00	$ 6.00	

where NofCases stands for the number of cases.

Thus, we want to find the number of cases that makes 4.80 NofCases = 240,000, which is 50,000. As long as the volume after the price increase does not drop below 50,000, we will be no worse off than we are now. If it doesn't drop that far, we will be better off.

	Now (000)	Just Cover (000)	(000)	(000)
Number of cases	60		NofCases	50
Revenue	$600		10.80 NofCases	$540
Variable cost	$360		− 6.00 NofCases	$300
GMC	$240	$240	4.80 NofCases	$240
Programmed marketing	$ 48	$ 48		$ 48
NMC	$192	$192		$192
Price per case	$10.00	$10.80		$10.80
Cost per case	$ 6.00			$ 6.00

The current volume is 60,000, and the just-cover volume is 50,000. So the implied just-cover volume is

$$\frac{60,000 - 50,000}{60,000} = 0.1667 \text{ or } 16.67\%$$

Either of these two methods—the reduction in units or the percentage reduction—tells us what we want to know. We will be no worse off unless volume drops below 50,000 cases; we will be no worse off unless volume drops by more than 16.7 percent.

This is simple enough to do. It becomes simpler with a formula.

Formula 2

$$\frac{\text{Percentage change}}{\text{in the just-cover point}} = -\frac{\text{Percentage change in price}}{\text{Percent GMC} + \text{Percentage change in price}}$$

In the example just above, the (proposed) percentage price increase is 8 percent (from $10 to $10.80), and the current GMC is 40 percent ($10 price, $6 variable cost, and $4 or 40 percent GMC). So,

$$\frac{\text{Percentage change}}{\text{in the just-cover point}} = -\frac{8}{40 + 8}$$

$$= -\frac{8}{48}$$

$$= -0.167 \text{ or } -16.7\%$$

Had the proposed increase been 5 percent, sales could fall $-5/(40 + 5)$, or 11 percent. And had it been a price decrease of (say) 7 percent, sales would have to increase by at least $-[-7/(40 + 7)] = 14.9$ percent, or we would be worse off than before.

To convert this percentage change in the just-cover point, simply multiply by the current volume:

Current volume -16.7%
Percentage change in the just-cover point $\times$ $\underline{60,000}$

Unit change in just-cover point $-10,000$ units

Formula 3

$$\frac{\text{Change in}}{\text{the JCP}} = \frac{\text{Percentage}}{\text{change in JCP}} \times \text{Current volume}$$

Formula 3 is pretty obvious.

Let me add a personal note. Formula 2 is one I use most. I remember it as P/PG, where P stands for percentage change in price and G stands for the percentage gross marketing contribution. I don't bother to remember the minus because I know in which direction the result must lie.

Simultaneous Changes in Programmed Costs

Let us imagine that the 8-percent increase is vetoed by the sales manager, but he agrees on a 5-percent increase plus an additional $12,000 a month in programmed costs to give the product a bit more consumer pull and the sales force a bit more push. Here are the figures:

	Now (000)		Just Covers the GMC (000)		Just Covers the NMC (000)	
Number of cases	60.00		53.33		56.00	
Revenue	$600	100.0%	$560	100.0%	$588	100.0%
Variable cost	$360	60.0%	$320	57.1%	$336	57.1%
GMC	$240	40.0%	$240	42.9%	$252	42.9%
Programmed marketing	$ 48		$ 60		$ 60	
NMC	$192		$180		$192	
Price per case	$10.00		$10.50		$10.50	
Cost per case	$ 6.00		$ 6.00		$ 6.00	
GMC per case	$ 4.00		$ 4.50		$ 4.50	

The first two columns of figures show where the product is now. The second two columns show the just-cover point that gives the same gross marketing contribution as we have now; namely that if sales do not fall below 53,330 cases (down from 60,000) the GMC will not decrease (below $240,000). The third two columns show the just-cover point to give the same net marketing contribution. They show that if sales do not fall below 56,000 cases, the NMC will not decrease (below $192,000).

From these three marketing control statements, it is easy to see how to reach the formula you need. The just-cover point for the GMC is figured as above,

$$\text{Percentage change in volume} = -\frac{\text{Percentage change in price}}{\text{Percentage GMC} + \text{Percentage change in price}}$$

$$= -\frac{5}{40 + 5}$$

$$= -0.111 \text{ or } -11.1\%$$

Thus, as long as volume drops no more than 11.1 percent, or 6,660 cases (11.1 percent of 60,000), we will be no worse off in terms of GMC.

But we would be worse off in terms of net marketing contribution; it would be $12,000 lower. So we have to sell more to just cover the extra $12,000. Since we have raised the price from $10 to $10.50, GMC per case has increased from $4.00 to $4.50, and the amount needed to just cover the extra $12,000 is $12,000/4.50 = 2,666$ cases.

The new JCP is found by adding these two:

Decrease in just-cover volume allowed by higher price	(6,666)
Increase in just-cover volume required by higher programmed costs	2,666
Total change in just-cover volume	(4,000)

As long as volume falls no more than 4,000 cases we will not suffer any reduction in net marketing contribution. Formally, the formulas are

Formula 4

$$\text{Percentage change in just-cover volume} = \text{Percentage change in volume because of price} + \text{Percentage change in volume because of programmed costs}$$

$$= \text{Formula 2} + \frac{\text{Change in programmed costs}}{\text{New unit GMC} \times \text{Initial volume}}$$

Formula 5

$$\text{Change in just-cover volume} = \text{Change in volume because of price} + \text{Change in volume because of programmed costs}$$

$$= \text{Formula 3} + \frac{\text{Change in programmed costs}}{\text{New unit GMC}}$$

What Formula 2 Means

Formula 2 is the basic relationship. Let's look at it more closely.

$$\text{Percentage change in the just-cover point} = - \frac{\text{Percentage change in price}}{\text{Percent GMC} + \text{Percentage change in price}}$$

In the example just above, the (proposed) percentage price increase is 8 percent, and the current GMC is 40 percent, so,

$$\text{Percentage change in the just-cover point} = - \frac{8}{40 + 8}$$

$$= -\frac{8}{48}$$

$$= -0.167 \text{ or } 16.7\%$$

The first thing to notice is that formula 2 deals with changes, changes in the just-cover point induced by changes in price. We are still dealing with marginal analysis.

Note the negative sign as well. Why is it there? Because as price goes up, the just-cover point must go down, and "go down" means that it must carry a negative sign.

Why is the change asymmetric? For example, an 8 percent increase in price (with a 40 percent GMC) leads to a JCP that is 16.7 percent lower, whereas an 8 percent decrease raises the JCP by only 25 percent. Why aren't the two the same? When you change the price you also change the unit gross marketing contribution, and any change in unit gross marketing contribution changes the JCP. A higher price increases the unit GMC and allows for a smaller drop in volume than at a lower price, which decreases the GMC. (Is this one reason why prices are "downward sticky"?)

Finally, note some qualitative relationships in the formula. Suppose the percentage GMC is large and the proposed price increase is small. Then formula 1 reduces to

$$\% \text{ change in JCP} \cong -\frac{\text{Small}}{\text{Large} + \text{Small}} \cong -\frac{1}{\text{Large}}$$

If the GMC is 60 percent and we are considering a small price change, say a few percentage points, the

$$\% \text{ change in JCP} \cong -\frac{1}{60} = -1.7\% \cong -2\%$$

Suppose both the percentage GMC and the proposed price decrease are roughly of the same order of magnitude. Then,

$$\% \text{ change in JCP} \cong -\frac{-\text{Small}}{\text{Small} + \text{Small}}$$

$$\cong +\frac{+\text{Small}}{2\ \text{Small}}$$

$$\cong \tfrac{1}{2} = 50\%$$

a whopping increase in the JCP.

HOW TO USE BREAK-EVEN AND JUST-COVER POINTS

1. If you don't already use BEPs or JCPs, start using them. They deepen the quality of a marketing analysis.

2. Don't expect too much of break-even analysis. It's a tool, a simple tool. Think of it more as shedding light on an issue rather than providing final answers.

3. Learn formulas 1 and 2, and practice using them. Try the others to see if they provide any help. If you expect to be at a meeting where price changes will be discussed, work out some just-cover points in advance. (Don't tell anyone how you do it. Just let them admire your brilliance.)

APPENDIX

One can lead a full rich life without knowing where mathematical formulas come from. But one or perhaps two readers may want to see the derivations of formula 1 and formula 2.

How Formula 1 Is Derived

The basic requirement is that gross market contribution be the same after the change as before. Let Q be the quantity currently being sold and G the current gross marketing contribution per unit. Let Q^* and G^* be the equivalent items after the proposal is carried out.

Because we are figuring a just-cover point, it must be that gross marketing contribution after the proposed program will be the same as it is now. That is,

$$Q^*G^* = QG$$

$$\frac{Q^*}{Q} = \frac{G}{G^*}$$

$$\frac{Q^*}{Q} - 1 = \frac{G}{G^*} - 1$$

$$\frac{Q^*}{Q} - \frac{Q}{Q} = \frac{G}{G^*} - \frac{G^*}{G^*}$$

$$\frac{Q^* - Q}{Q} = \frac{G - G^*}{G^*}$$

This says that the percentage change in quantity (the left-hand side) equals $(G - G^*)/G^*$, which is formula 1.

How Formula 2 Is Derived

We start with current operations: we sell Q units of a product at price P and unit cost C. So,

$$\text{Revenue} = PQ$$

$$\text{Costs} = CQ$$

and

$$\text{Gross marketing contribution} = PQ - CQ = (P - C)Q$$

The proposal is to (say) increase the price to P^*. Unit cost will not change but buyers will buy less. The question is how much less before gross marketing contribution suffers.

Let Q^* represent the just-cover point that we want to solve for. That is, we raise the price to P^* and sales drop to Q^*, then the gross marketing contribution will not change.

$$\frac{\text{GMC before}}{(P - C)Q} = \frac{\text{GMC proposed}}{(P^* - C)Q^*} \tag{1}$$

The rest of this appendix is a mechanical working out of this equation.

There is one last addition. Microeconomists and other mathematicians use the symbol Δ to mean "change in." Thus, we read Δvolume as "change in volume." Since the proposed price is merely the current price plus a change in the current price, we can represent the proposed price like this:

$$
\begin{array}{ccccc}
\text{Proposed price} & = & \text{Current price} & + & \text{Change in current price} \\
P^* & = & P & + & \Delta P
\end{array} \tag{2}
$$

and in like fashion

$$
\begin{array}{ccccc}
\text{Just-cover volume} & = & \text{Current volume} & + & \text{Change in current volume} \\
Q^* & = & Q & + & \Delta Q
\end{array} \tag{3}
$$

The recipe is as follows: Mix equations (1), (2), and (3) together, shake well, and pour out formula 2.

$Q(P - C) = Q^*(P^* - C)$	Equation 1 again
$\quad = (Q + \Delta Q)(P^* - C)$	Substitute in equation (3)
$QP - QC = QP^* - QC + P^*\Delta Q - C\Delta Q$	Grind away
$QP = QP^* + P^*\Delta Q - C\Delta Q$	Drop equal terms
$QP = Q(P + \Delta P) + (P + \Delta P)\Delta Q - C\Delta Q$	Substitute in equation (2)

$$QP = QP + Q\Delta P + P\Delta Q + \Delta P\Delta Q - C\Delta Q \qquad \text{More grinding}$$

$$0 = Q\Delta P + P\Delta Q + \Delta P\Delta Q - C\Delta Q \qquad \text{Drop equal terms}$$

$$-P\Delta Q - \Delta P\Delta Q + C\Delta Q = Q\Delta P \qquad \text{Move terms}$$

$$\Delta Q(-P - \Delta P + C) = Q\Delta P \qquad \text{Factor out } \Delta Q$$

$$\frac{\Delta Q}{Q}(-P - \Delta P + C) = \Delta P \qquad \text{Divide through by } Q$$

$$\frac{\Delta Q}{Q} = \frac{\Delta P}{-P + C - \Delta P} \qquad \begin{array}{l}\text{Divide through by}\\ -P - \Delta P + C\end{array}$$

$$\frac{\Delta Q}{Q} = -\frac{\Delta P}{P - C + \Delta P} \cdot \frac{1/P}{1/P} \qquad \begin{array}{l}\text{Multiply the top and the}\\ \text{bottom by } 1/P\end{array}$$

$$\boxed{\frac{\Delta Q}{Q} = -\frac{\Delta P/P}{(P - C)/P + \Delta P/P}}$$

that is

$$\% \text{ change in volume} = -\frac{\% \text{ of change in price}}{\% \text{ GMC} + \% \text{ change in price}}$$

NOTE

1. My rule is this: Don't split an infinitive unless what you get is ungainly. In that case, split or rewrite. To my ear "to just cover" reads better than "just to cover" or as I have it here "to cover, just."

Chapter 8

Contribution Analysis—Why Didn't We Make Plan?

We have seen how gross marketing contribution and net marketing contribution can help a manager make better decisions. Contribution can also help control a marketing program. The subject of this chapter is using contribution to control marketing programs.

The general procedure for controlling anything is so familiar that it merits little discussion: you plan a program, set targets in terms of gross marketing contribution (GMC) and net marketing contribution (NMC), execute the program, compare the results with the targets, and based on this comparison, lay new plans and set new targets.

This chapter focuses on the comparison of targets with results. It describes a tried and true method from cost accounting—variance analysis—for understanding what went wrong (or occasionally what went right). Microeconomic theory provides no underpinnings for what is discussed here, which means that variance analysis is neither so appealing or so obvious to the untutored mind. But just as with previous material in this book, once understood it throws a good deal of light on what has happened to a marketing program.

Before you read this chapter check the battery in your calculator. You will understand things better if you check the figures as you go along.

In each of the examples that follow, I will show how variance analysis is done. I will also show that a garden variety analysis of changes in contribution is often sufficient. Before I explain variance analysis, let us look at two examples to set the scene.

TWO EXAMPLES TO GET STARTED

A Simple Example

Let us start with a simple example. Here are planned and actual figures side by side. What we want to do is figure out why we missed the plan by $3,800.

	Planned	Actual	Difference
Volume sold, in pounds	70,000	74,000	4,000
Price per pound	$1.80	$1.70	$0.10
Variable cost per pound	$0.90	$0.90	—
Unit gross marketing contribution	$0.90	$0.80	$(0.10)
Sales	$126,000	$125,800	$(200)
Variable costs	$ 63,000	$ 66,600	$(3,600)
Gross marketing contribution	$ 63,000	$ 59,200	$(3,800)

Because variance analysis can get messy (for anyone who does not work with it regularly), keep your common sense turned on. Here it is clear that although we sold more pounds, prices weakened and GMC fell. The decrease in GMC must reflect the interplay of two factors—the increased pounds, which should increase it, and decreased price, which should decrease it.

But how do the two interact? Which is the larger? Can you tell before you go on?

Yes. At least one can make some sensible guesses. We sold four thousand more pounds than we planned. Had we gotten our full unit GMC of $0.90, we would have made an extra 4,000 × $0.90 = $3,600. But the total GMC fell by $3,800 instead. So the effect of the lower unit GMC was large enough to offset the $3,600 due to extra sales *and* decrease the total by another $3,800. It must be 7,400 because

$$\$3,600 + \$(7,400) = \$(3,800)$$

Be sure you understand what these two numbers mean. Because we sold more pounds than planned, our total GMC should have risen. This is called a *volume variance*. It is that portion of the change in GMC that was caused by the change in sales volume. For some reason—costs crept up or prices softened—the unit GMC fell. Because it fell, total GMC is down. This is called a *contribution variance*. It is the portion of the change in GMC that was caused by the change in unit contribution. In this example, it would be clearer to call this a price variance.

Volume variance	$ 3,600
Price variance	(7,400)
Net change in gross marketing contribution	(3,800)

We have broken down the net change into its components, and in the process concluded that the fall in unit GMC was the principal cause of the fall in the overall GMC.

Decomposition of the Net Change in Gross Marketing Contribution

---

Differences Due to Change in Unit GMC

Actual GMC   = Actual volume × Actual unit GMC
         =   74,000   × $0.80   = $59,200
Planned GMC = Actual volume × Planned unit GMC
         =   74,000   × $0.90   = 66,600

Decrease in GMC due to failure to
  get planned unit GMC $(7,400)

Differences Due to Change in Volume

Actual GMC   = Planned volume × Planned unit GMC
         =   74,000   × $0.90   = $66,600
Planned GMC = Actual volume   × Planned unit GMC
         =   70,000   × $0.90   = 63,000

Increase in GMC due to success in
  selling more than planned   3,600
Net change in GMC $(3,800)

Second Example

Here are the results for the month of March shown in marketing control statement (MCS).

MCS 1

	Planned (000)	Actual (000)	Difference (000)
Sales	$600.0	$640.0	$ 40.0
Discounts and allowances	30.0	50.0	(20.0)
Net sales	570.0	590.0	20.0
Cost of goods sold	288.0	326.5	(38.5)
Gross marketing contribution	282.0	263.5	(18.5)
Programmed marketing costs	43.8	43.8	
Net marketing contribution	238.2	219.7	(18.5)

The Common Sense Analysis. A glance gives us both the good news and the bad news. Sales are up by $40,000, but NMC is down $18,500. The causes are not so clear, but discounts and allowances are up, presumably because we had to shave our prices, and cost of goods sold is also up, pushing GMC down. These don't explain much, however, because sales

are up, and as sales go up we expect both discounts and cost of goods sold
to increase.

The first commonsense step is to percentage the figures.

MCS 2

	(000)		**(000)**	
Sales	$600.0	100.0%	$640.0	100.0%
Discounts and allowances	30.0	5.0	50.0	7.8
Net sales	570.0	95.0	590.0	92.2
Cost of goods sold	288.0	48.0	326.5	51.0
Gross marketing contribution	282.0	47.0	263.5	41.2
Programmed marketing costs	43.8	7.3	43.8	6.8
Net marketing contribution	238.2	39.7	219.7	34.3

Now things are clearer (although the last column doesn't quite add due to
rounding). Discounts and allowances have risen faster than sales have, so
they have increased as a percentage of sales. The same is true of the cost
of goods sold. As a result, the GMC has fallen from 47 percent of sales to
41 percent (rounded). We've made progress, but we still don't have a feel
for whether discounts or cost of goods sold was more important.

Discounts and allowances should have been 5 percent of $640,000 but
were 7.8 percent. So we can get an estimate of how much the price
shaving cost us.

	(000)
Planned discounts and allowances (planned at 5 percent of sales)	$30
What discounts and allowances would have been at the higher sales level if they had been 5 percent of sales ($640 × 0.05)	32
Decrease in NMC due to higher discounts	(2)

Part of the reason NMC is down $18,500 is that we shaved prices $2,000
more than we had planned to.

In a similar fashion, we can compare what cost of goods sold should
have been at the planned 48 percent of sales and what it was.

	(000)
Planned cost of goods sold (COGS) (planned at 48 percent of sales)	$288.0

What COGS would have been at the higher
sales level if COGS had continued at 48 per-
cent ($640 × 0.48)   307.2

Decrease in NMC due to increase in COGS   (19.2)

This suggests that the increase in cost of goods sold was much more
important in pushing down the NMC than shaving the price. But it is only
a suggestion, because the two explanations literally do not add up.

	(000)
Price shaving variance	$ (2.0)
COGS variance	(19.2)
Total variance explained by commonsense analysis	$(21.2)
Actual difference in NMC	$(18.5)

Although we are on pretty solid ground in saying that the increase in cost
of goods sold was the chief reason NMC fell, the sum of the commonsense explanations does not equal the decrease in NMC.

VARIANCE ANALYSIS

Variance analysis offers a formal way to tackle the problem of explaining why what happened happened. As it is typically used, variance analysis breaks down the change in net marketing contribution into three
areas—sales volume, price, and product mix—and the three do add to the
total change in net marketing contribution. You end up with a summary
that says this:

Change in NMC = Volume variance + Price variance + Product mix variance

The general approach is the same as just outlined. You compare what was
planned with what would have happened if some ratio, price, or unit cost
hadn't changed as it did. Let us continue with the second example.

Volume Variance

One of the reasons NMC declined was that sales changed. Or more to
the point, we must explain the irritating fact that sales went up but NMC
went down. We can start by looking at the *volume variance,* which tells us
what would have happened to NMC if we had achieved the GMC percentage we had planned to. That is, we start by pretending that the marketing
control statement looks like this:

MCS 3

---

	(000)		
Sales	$640.0	100.00%	Actual sales
Discounts and allowances	32.0	5.00	← Planned discounts per-
Net sales	608.0	95.00	centage
Cost of goods sold	307.2	48.00	← Planned COGS percentage
Gross marketing contribution	300.8	47.00	← Planned GMC percentage
Programmed marketing costs	43.8	6.84	
	257.0	40.16	

There is no label on the last line. Can you supply it? Just what is that $257,000? It is the net marketing contribution that we would have gotten (1) given actual sales and (2) if we had been right on plan with both discounts and allowances and cost of goods sold.

The planned GMC was 47 percent of sales. Sales increased by $40,000. If nothing else had changed, NMC would have gone up by 0.47 × 40,000 = $18,800. This is the volume variance:

$$\text{Volume variance} = \$18,800$$

Incidentally not everyone calls this a volume variance. Some managers call it a marketing variance on the grounds that it measures how the market has reacted to the firm's marketing effort.

Product Mix Variance

A second possible cause of the decline in NMC is problems with the product mix. We might have sold more products with low GMCs and fewer products with high GMCs than we planned. If so, the NMC would be depressed.

The planned mix of products was such that we expected our gross marketing contribution to be 47 percent of sales—but in fact it was a good deal lower, 41.2 percent. But we want to separate the effect of the product mix from the effect that price shaving had. So, for the mix variance, we will pretend that we did not have to shave price, which means we keep discounts and allowances at 5 percent of sales. This means the marketing control statement would have looked like this:

MCS 4

	(000)		
Sales	$640.0	100.00%	Actual sales
Discounts and allowances	32.0	5.00	← Planned discounts
Net sales	608.0	95.00	percentage
Cost of goods sold	326.5	51.02	← Actual COGS dollars
Gross marketing contribution	281.5	43.98	← Actual product mix
Programmed marketing costs	43.8	6.84	percentage
Net marketing contribution	237.7	37.14	

In the previous marketing control statement, MCS 3, the GMC was $300,800. In MCS 4, it is $281,500, a difference of $(19,300). If prices had not been shaved:

	(000)
Actual sales	$640.0
Planned discounts and allowances (@ 5%)	32.0
Expected net sales without any price shaving	608.0
What cost of goods sold would have been if product mix hadn't changed (@ 48%)	307.2
What GMC would have been had neither the product mix changed nor prices been shaved	300.8
What GMC would have been given the actual product mix but assuming no price shaving	281.5
Decrease in GMC due to changes in the product mix	(19.3)

This is the product mix variance. It is the difference between the GMC at the planned product mix and the GMC at the actual product mix (assuming no price shaving).

Price Variance

Finally we have that proportion of the change in GMC that is due solely to shaving the price. We look at our final marketing control statement, MCS 5, which is nothing more than the actual results we got—actual volume, actual discounts and allowances (which means actual prices), and actual product mix. (This simply repeats part of MCS 1.)

MCS 5

	Actual (000)
Sales	$640.0
Discounts and allowances	50.0
Net sales	590.0
Standard COGS	326.5
Gross marketing contribution	263.5
Programmed marketing costs	43.8
Net marketing contribution	219.7

The price variance is actual net sales less what net sales would have been had prices stayed as planned—that is, had prices been such that net sales equalled 95 percent of gross sales.

	Net Sales (000)
Actual	$590.0
Planned (0.95 × 640)	608.0
Price variance	(18.0)

Summing Up

We have calculated three variances that help us better understand the decline in gross marketing contribution.

		(000)
Planned gross marketing contribution		$238.2
Volume variance	$18.8	
Mix variance	(19.3)	
Price variance	(18.0)	(18.5)
Actual gross marketing contribution		219.7

In this example, volume, mix, and price effects all contributed about equally: higher sales *volume* acted to increase GMC while a poorer product *mix* and some *price* shaving acted to decrease GMC. The manager is now in a position to formulate a new plan that builds on a deeper understanding of what went wrong and what went right.

Here is a second summary of the same example:

Column:	1	2	3	4
Volume:	Planned	Actual	Actual	Actual
Mix:	Planned	Planned	Actual	Actual
Price:	Planned	Planned	Planned	Actual
Sales	$600.0	$640.0	$640.0	$640.0
Discounts and allowances	30.0	32.0	32.0	50.0
Net sales	570.0	608.0	608.0	590.0
Standard COGS	288.0	307.2	326.5	326.5
Gross marketing contribution	282.0	300.8	281.5	263.5
Programmed marketing costs	43.8	43.8	43.8	43.8
Net marketing contribution	238.2	257.0	237.7	219.7

As we move from column 1 to column 4, one aspect changes each time. Column 1 is the planned MCS. Column 2 contains the MCS we would have gotten at actual sales, but with prices and the product mix just as planned. Column 3 contains the MCS we would have gotten at actual sales and actual product mix, but with prices just as planned. Column 4 contains the MCS we got, period.

An alternative way of looking at these four marketing control statements is to reduce them to percentages of gross sales.

Column:	1	2	3	4
Volume:	Planned	Actual	Actual	Actual
Mix:	Planned	Planned	Actual	Actual
Price:	Planned	Planned	Planned	Actual
Sales (000)	$600.0	$640.0	$640.0	$640.0
Sales	100.00%	100.00%	100.00%	100.00%
Discounts and allowances	5.00	5.00	5.00	7.81
Net sales	95.00	95.00	95.00	92.19
Standard COGS	48.00	48.00	51.02	51.02
Gross marketing contribution	47.00	47.00	43.98	41.17
Programmed marketing costs	7.30	6.84	6.84	6.84
Net marketing contribution	39.70	40.16	37.14	34.33

The key difference between each successive pair of columns is highlighted. Column 1 assumes planned sales ($600.0), while column 2 contains actual sales ($640.0). Column 2 assumes the planned product mix (with a GMC of 47 percent), while column 3 contains the actual GMC percentage (43.98). Column 3 assumes planned discounts and allowances (5 percent) while column 4 contains actual discounts and allowances (7.81 percent).

Let us return to the four columns discussed, which are repeated here:

Column:	1	2	3	4
Volume:	Planned	Actual	Actual	Actual
Mix:	Planned	Planned	Actual	Actual
Price:	Planned	Planned	Planned	Actual
Sales	$600.0	$640.0	$640.0	$640.0
Discounts and allowances	30.0	32.0	32.0	50.0
Net sales	570.0	608.0	608.0	590.0
Standard COGS	288.0	307.2	326.5	326.5
Gross marketing contribution	282.0	300.8	281.5	263.5
Programmed marketing costs	43.8	43.8	43.8	43.8
Net marketing contribution	238.2	257.0	237.7	219.7

Let us work with only the four net marketing contributions at the bottom. The difference between each pair of NMCs is one of the variances.

	(000)	
NMC in the second column	$257.0	
− NMC in the first column	238.2	
Volume variance		$ 18.8
NMC in the third column	237.7	
− NMC in the second column	257.0	
Product mix variance		(19.3)
NMC in the last column	219.7	
− NMC in the third column	237.7	
Price variance		(18.0)
Total Variance		(18.5)

VARIANCE ANALYSIS—ANOTHER PASS

The fundamental idea behind variance analysis is easy to understand, namely that we compare what did happen with what might have happened if one or more factors had not changed. But it is not so easy to remember (say) the difference between a volume variance and a mix variance, particularly for the marketers for whom this book is written, marketers without an accounting background or those like me who took accounting, once, some time ago. (Just how long is nobody's business.) So it is worthwhile taking a second look at the three variances.

Let us imagine a firm that sells three product lines, Petite, Average, and Jumbo. Here is the plan for the next month.

Products	Units (000)	Proportion of Sales	Prices (*a*)	Variable Costs (*b*)	Unit GMC (*c* = *a* − *b*)	Unit GMC minus Ave. UGMC (*c* − **$5.30**)
Petite	150	0.300	$10.00	$ 6.00	$4.00	($1.30)
Average	250	0.500	25.00	18.00	7.00	1.70
Jumbo	100	0.200	12.00	9.00	3.00	(2.30)
	500	1.000	Average unit GMC		$5.30	

Abbreviated Marketing Control Statement

	(000)
Sales	$8,950
Var. Costs	6,300
GMC	2,650
Average Unit GMC	$5.30

Volume variance tells us what happens when volume changes but the product mix, embodied in the column headed "Proportions of Sales" stays the same, and prices stay the same. Imagine that volume increases 10 percent across the board, but that neither mix nor prices change.

	Planned Volume	Volume After a 10-Percent Increase
Petite	150	165
Average	250	275
Jumbo	100	110
	500	550

Then the actual figures would look like this:

Products	Units (000)	Proportion	Prices	Var. Costs	Unit GMC	Unit GMC minus Ave. UGMC
Petite	165	0.300	$10.00	$ 6.00	$4.00	($1.30)
Average	275	0.500	25.00	18.00	7.00	1.70
Jumbo	110	0.200	12.00	9.00	3.00	(2.30)
	550	1.000				

Abbreviated Marketing Control Statement

	Planned (000)	Actual (000)	Difference (000)
Sales	$8,950	$9,845	$895
Variable costs	6,300	6,930	(630)
GMC	2,650	2,915	265
Average unit GMC	5.30	5.18	

And the volume variance is simply the difference between planned GMC and actual GMC = $2,915,000 − $2,650,000 = $265,000, which of course is 10 percent of planned GMC.

An alternative way of calculating a volume variance is to calculate a variance for each product and add them together.

	Volume Actual (a) (000)	Volume Planned (b) (000)	Difference $(c = a − b)$ (000)	Unit GMC (d) (000)	Variance Term $(d \times c)$ (000)
Petite	165	150	15	$4.00	$ 60
Average	275	250	25	7.00	175
Jumbo	110	100	10	3.00	30
	550	500	50		$265

Again, the total volume variance is $265,000.[1]

The plan calls for 30 percent of unit sales to be in Petites, 50 percent in Averages, and 20 percent in Jumbos, and for the average unit GMC to be $5.30. What this means is this: If we sell in the planned proportion of 30:50:20, then on average an extra "unit" of sales will yield $5.30 in gross marketing contribution. Both Petites and Jumbos bring in low unit GMCs, $4 and $3 a unit, respectively. If the mix shifts so that we sell more of these and less of the Average line, total GMC will suffer. But if more than half the units sold are Averages, with their high unit GMC, total GMC will increase.

The mix variance tells what happens when the product mix changes but not prices or volume. In the following figures Petites make up a higher proportion of sales than planned and Averages a smaller proportion. And since Petites have a smaller unit GMC, the total GMC is down, as is the average unit GMC.

Products	Units (000)	Proportion	Prices	Variable Costs	Unit GMC	Unit GMC minus Average Unit GMC
Petite	170	0.340	$10.00	$ 6.00	$4.00	($1.18)
Average	230	0.460	25.00	18.00	7.00	1.82
Jumbo	100	0.200	12.00	9.00	3.00	(2.18)
	500	1.000				

Abbreviated Marketing Control Statement

	Planned (000)	Actual (000)	Difference (000)
Sales	$8,950	$8,650	$(300)
Variable costs	6,300	6,060	240
GMC	2,650	2,590	(60)
Average unit GMC	5.30	5.18	

The mix variance is actual GMC minus planned GMC, or $2,590,000 − 2,650,000 = ($60,000).

But there are other ways of figuring the mix variance as well. One way involves multiplying the change in unit volume for each product by the difference between the products' unit GMC and the planned average unit GMC. When reading this it seems complicated, but as we work through the figures it will become clear.

Product	Volume Actual (a) (000)	Volume Planned (b) (000)	Volume Difference (c = a − b) (000)	Planned Unit GMC (d)	Planned Average Unit GMC (e)	Unit GMC Difference (f = d − e)	Mix Variance (c × f) (000)
Petite	170	150	20	$4.00	$5.30	$(1.30)	$(26)
Average	230	250	(20)	7.00	5.30	1.70	(34)
Jumbo	100	100	0	3.00	5.30	(2.30)	0
							(60)

The numbers in the last column tell us a fair amount. Petites are a low GMC item for this company. But instead of selling 150,000 units as it had planned, the company sold 170,000. It sold *more* of its low contribution product—chalk one up against the company to the tune of $26,000. Averages generate the highest GMC but the firm sold fewer of them. Another chalk mark, this time for $34,000. The mix we sold is distinctly poorer than what we had planned.

The price variance tells us what happens when prices change but both volume and mix are unchanged. We might imagine that we raise prices 10 percent on all three products without losing any volume or changing the mix.

Products	Units (000)	Proportion	Prices	Variable Costs	Unit GMC	Unit GMC minus Average UGMC
Petite	150	0.300	$11.00	$ 6.00	$5.00	($2.09)
Average	250	0.500	27.50	18.00	9.50	2.41
Jumbo	100	0.200	13.20	9.00	4.20	(2.89)
	500	1.000				

Abbreviated Marketing Control Statement

	Planned (000)	Actual (000)	Difference (000)
Sales	$8,950	$9,845	$895
Variable costs	6,300	6,300	—
GMC	2,650	3,545	895
Average unit GMC	5.30	7.09	

The price variance is the difference between the actual and planned gross marketing contribution, or $3,545,000 − $2,650,000 = $895,000.

Just as there are alternative ways of figuring the volume and mix variances, there are alternative ways of figuring the price variance. Here is one. Price variance is the actual volume times the difference between actual and planned selling prices.

Product	Actual Volume (a)	Selling Prices Actual (b)	Selling Prices Planned (c)	Price Difference ($d = b - c$)	Price Variance ($a \times d$)
Petite	150	$11.00	$10.00	$1.00	$150
Average	250	27.50	25.00	2.50	625
Jumbo	100	13.20	12.00	1.20	120
Total price variance					895

VARIANCES FOR MARKET SIZE AND MARKET SHARE

If a brand's fate is in the laps of the gods, that is, if its fate is affected by what happens to overall demand and the brand's share of market, then it makes sense to add these factors to your variance analysis. The same kind of thinking—decomposing a change into its components by comparing what did happen with what might have happened—can be applied to changes in share and market size. These changes can be decomposed into changes in market size and changes in market share.[2]

The idea is straightforward. Every marketer knows that gains or losses of market share need to be considered in the light of changes in the size of the market.

Suppose a company planned to hold its 5.5 percent share of an industry market of 6,000,000 units. Thus, it plans to sell $0.055 \times 6,000,000 = 330,000$ units. It does sell 330,000 units, but at the end of the period it discovers that the market has grown 10 percent to 6,600,000, and that it did not maintain its share. Its share fell to $330,000/6,600,000 = 0.05$, or 5 percent.

We can decompose this change into a share variance and a size variance.

Market Size Variance

This variance is the value of the change in industry sales if the planned share is obtained. Value here means the value at the planned unit gross marketing contribution.

	(000)
Actual industry sales (units)	6,600
Planned industry sales (units)	6,000
Changes in industry sales	600
Increase in unit sales if we had held share, 5.5% of 600	33
Times planned unit gross marketing contribution	× $ 16
Market size variance	$528

The market size variance is $528,000. The gross marketing contribution is $528,000 higher than it would have been had the market size not increased.

Market Share Variance

The market size variance assumes share is held constant (at the planned value). The market share variance assumes that market size remains unchanged, but this time at actual volume.

The market share variance answers this question, Given the actual size of the industry, what effect did the change in market share have on gross marketing contribution? The computations are as follows:

Actual market share	5.0%
Less planned market share	−5.5
Change in market share	(0.5)
Times actual industry sales	×6,600
Equals	(33)
Times planned unit gross marketing contribution	× 16
Market share variance	$(528)

The market share variance is ($528,000), and the firm's gross marketing contribution is $528,000 lower than it would have been had the firm held onto its share as it planned to.

A WRAP-UP

Variance analysis will not solve many of the problems that marketers face. It is most useful for giving a manager a deeper understanding of what went wrong (or occasionally what went right), and thus it serves as a basis for doing better. Thus it serves best in controlling the marketing operation.

The focus of variance analysis is the short run—this month's results against the plan, this quarter's results against the plan. That is, it deals with tactics. And it is an inward looking measure. It is of little value in making fundamental decisions that affect the course of the entire business. These must be based on overall strategy and a reading of the environment.

Some writers on accounting fault variance analysis on the grounds that it does not reveal underlying causes. It does not say why a variance is large or small or why volume exceeded budget. We might have an unfavorable sales variance not because of problems with the sales force but because the plan was too optimistic.

This objection holds no water, even though it is correct. On the same grounds, a physician would not use a thermometer because it does not provide a diagnosis. But thermometers have advantages in spite of their inability to diagnose—they are cheap, they are reliable, they are portable, and they provide an important piece of information. Thermometers measure symptoms; doctors diagnose.

This is just how one should think of variance analysis. It does not answer fundamental questions. Only a manager can do that. But it is cheap and it provides some useful information on symptoms.

There is a small technical problem with variance analysis as well. Variances are often calculated in a sequence—first this one, then the next, finally the last. But in a different sequence, the variances might well change their values. To use a cumbrous phrase from academia, they are not uniquely defined. To a professor this can be a difficulty. To a manager, it means to pay less attention to the exact size of the variance and more attention to its order of magnitude and whether it is favorable or unfavorable.[3]

The Poor Man's Approach to Contribution Analysis

In the examples in this chapter, several times I have percentaged planned and actual figures and compared the percentages. There is nothing deep or astute in such a step, but it can prove fruitful when you are trying to understand what went wrong.

HOW TO USE CONTRIBUTION ANALYSIS

1. If you have come up through the marketing ranks, variance analysis may be new to you. That is all the more reason to try it. Try it first on simple situations concerning your own products. By "simple" I mean simple enough to do by hand, following the examples in the chapter.

If you like the results of the trial, try it on a more complex or realistic situation.

2. Be on your guard. Variance analysis can get messy. *Think* about what the analysis tells you. What it says should look sensible in terms of what you know about your customers, your markets, and your industry.

3. Because it is messy, variance analysis calls for a pro, an accountant who can structure the analysis. If you find it useful, you will have to call on an accountant to do the dirty work. To repeat, variance analysis is messy.

If you insist on doing it yourself, plan to do some reading and a lot of number pushing before you get it straight.[4]

4. Variance analysis is most helpful if you think in terms of orders of magnitude, not precise magnitudes. Suppose this is the result of an analysis

Price variance	(16)
Volume variance	32
Mix variance	8
Change in net marketing contribution	24

Don't conclude that the influence of volume on NMC was four times that of mix. Instead conclude that (1) volume was a lot more important than mix in explaining the increase in NMC and (2) price (with a negative sign) was somewhere between them in importance.

NOTES

1. There is another way to get the volume variance:

$$\text{Volume variance} = \frac{\text{Total change in}}{\text{number of units}} \times \frac{\text{Average unit gross}}{\text{marketing contribution}}$$

$$= \quad 50,000 \quad \times \text{\$5.30}$$

$$= \quad \text{\$265,000}$$

2. For more on these variances see J. Shank and N. Churchill, "Variance analysis: a management-oriented approach," *Accounting Review* (Oct. 1977), 955.

3. It also means that once having adopted a sequence for doing variance analysis, you should stick to it.

4. A few sources to start with are Charles T. Horngren and George Foster, *Cost Accounting, A Managerial Emphasis,* 7th edition (Englewood Cliffs, N.J.: Prentice-Hall, 1991), Chapter 26; Robert F. Lusch and William F. Bentz, "A Marketing-Accounting Framework for Controlling Product Profitability," *Management Accounting* (January 1980), 17–25; James E. Hulbert and Norman E. Toy, "A Strategic Framework for Marketing Control," *Journal of Marketing,* Vol. 41 (April 1977), 12–21.

Chapter 9

Last Words

Here is what I have said in this book.

Commit yourself to learning some microeconomics. If you do, expect to see to the heart of some of the problems that come across your desk more easily and more quickly. But don't expect a great deal. Nothing as abstract as microeconomics can provide very much help.

Focus your energies more on understanding the behavior of costs in your business. That means, at the least, learning to tell variable costs from fixed costs from programmed costs. Even if you have never had an accounting course, you can in time, if you apply yourself, learn about accounting and your costs. Understanding costs is a key to understanding a great deal of what is really important in marketing (and in business).

Be on the lookout for costs that don't show up on financial statements. Opportunity costs and imputed costs are real costs and cost real money. Understand what sunk costs are all about and use your understanding to good effect.

Learn enough about the business of your distributors—retailers, whole-salers, jobbers, reps, whoever—to see their business from their point of view, from their financial point of view. If you use distributors and don't have their financial information at your fingertips—things like profits as a percentage of sales, gross margins, turnover, and sales per square foot—plan to do better.

Get savvy about averages. Don't be gulled by a misleading average, and remember that behind each average is a spread of values, from smallest to largest. Above all, don't confuse average values and marginal values. They are not the same.

Take the central tenet of marginal analysis as a basic operating procedure in your marketing programs. That is, focus on things that change, and don't spend more on something than it is worth. But as with anything as general as this, don't expect marginal analysis to lead to a richer, fuller life, or even to ease and wealth. Like any tool, marginal analysis has its uses. But it will not solve all your marketing problems.

Adopt the basic form of the marketing control statement. You should know, for your most important programs, how much gross marketing contribution and net marketing contribution each generates. And if you do enjoy, perhaps for the first time, really understanding the cash flows produced by your marketing programs.

Break-even points and just-cover points are simple, easy to use, easy to understand, and of substantial help to a marketer in an uncertain world. Try the formulas in this chapter at least a few times. Not everyone finds them useful, but many do.

It is useful to decompose changes in gross marketing contribution. But to a marketer it can get messy. As with the formulas dealing with break-even points, you should at least try some analysis of gross marketing contribution before you give up on this idea. It can be quite useful.

Appendixes

PROBLEMS

WHY ALL THESE PROBLEMS?

Because you learn best by doing.

Problems are like practicing scales on the piano. Dreary, perhaps, but they nimble your fingers and teach you fingering that you will use; and piano pieces, real music, are filled with scales and bits of scales, so in learning scales you are learning something practical. Above all, scales give you facility. You can't learn to play the piano by reading about playing.

The elementary problems that follow may seem dreary too. But they teach you the thinking and number pushing that you need; and elementary as they are, they do form part of any standard marketing analysis. Above all, they will give you facility. You can't learn to push the numbers by reading about it. Because these problems are not difficult, the answers are straightforward.

The slightly more difficult problems are tougher because you have to do some guessing and you have to draw on what you know about business and marketing. The answers to these problems are rewarding, I think, because they show how you can approach practical problems.

Neither set of problems should be a chore. No one is looking over your shoulder. My suggestion is: keep doing the problems until you get bored or they no longer challenge you.

Chapter 2

Questions on Microeconomics

1. From time to time, microeconomists argue the value of a product in terms of its market reception. They call it the "test of the market." For example,

there are elaborate mathematical models of the economy, such as those sold by DRI and other economic consulting firms, that have passed the test of the market. The argument seems to be that because people will pay, the product is valuable.

Can you think of counter examples where (1) something of value does not pass the test of the market, and (2) where something that is valueless does pass? Now consider this question: Does microeconomics itself pass the test of the market?

2.   Microeconomists do not seem to be conspicuously happier or more serene or richer than any one else. Yet presumably, they know a great deal more about maximizing utility than any one else.

How would they reply?

Chapter 3

General Questions on Costs

1.   Is the following a good summary of the difference between variable and fixed costs? If not, in what respects is it not?

Variable costs are the costs of doing business, while fixed costs are the costs of being in business.

2.   "Since all costs vary in the long run, it would be more accurate not to use the phrase *fixed costs* but rather to use *costs fixed in the short run.*"

Comment, ignoring the indigestibility of the proposed phrase.

3.   I buy (say) one thousand pounds sterling when the price in U.S. dollars is $1.10 per pound. While I hold the pounds, the price rises to $2.00. I am delighted that I got a good deal. I begin to plan my trip to England when a spasm of microeconomic analysis overtakes me.

I have no decision to make. I am going to England and I will spend the money. But how much will the trip cost me? The value of my thousand pounds is the value of the next best thing I can do with them, which is use them to buy dollars. The value of that is 1,000 x $2.00 = $2,000. According to the opportunity cost principle, if I spend the pounds in England as I plan to, the cost will be $2,000, not $1,100. I am not delighted any longer.

The conclusion seems clear: it does not pay to buy foreign currency when it is cheap.

If this is the incorrect analysis, *why* is it incorrect? If this is the incorrect analysis what is the correct analysis?

Questions on Cost Classification

1. When they apply every three years to the Federal Communications Commission to have their licenses renewed, radio and television stations promise to devote a certain (small) proportion of their air time to public and community service. For example, most stations commit to broadcasting each day or each week a certain number of public service announcements (PSAs), which are free advertisements for non-profit organizations. One station might, for example, commit to broadcasting six PSAs a day, another to one an hour, a third to broadcasting at least fifty a week.

    Do the stations incur any costs in doing this? If they do, what kind of costs are they?

2. A remanufacturer renovates used products and resells them. For example, he might take a used, gasoline-powered weed cutter, inspect it, disassemble the motor and drive shafts, clean them, replace the worn parts or rebuild them, install new fittings, repaint the housing, reassemble the weed cutter, and test it. He now has a weed cutter that he sells for perhaps 60 percent of the cost of a new weed cutter. Thus a remanufactured weed cutter that might sell new for $150 would sell at $90.

    One of the problems facing a remanufacturer is getting "cores," the term used to describe the used product. Once a remanufacturer is in business, he gets most of his cores by taking trade-ins from his customers. But when he is just starting, he has no customers. Where can he get cores, if he is not able to buy enough in the open market? Some solve this problem by buying *new* weed cutters and selling them as *remanufactured,* deliberately losing money on each sale so as to generate a supply of trade-ins. What kind of a cost is this?

3. IBM introduced the PC Jr in November 1983. Despite an introductory budget estimated at some $40 million, sales started slow and stayed low. One of the fix-ups that IBM tried was changing terms to dealers. Instead of normal terms of sale, IBM allowed dealers to delay payments for the PC Jr six months longer than usual.

    In doing this, IBM incurred a cost. What kind?

4. Here are two examples of competitive buy-outs.

    In Australia, where it is difficult to close a bank account, banks wooing
    new customers may offer to close accounts in their old banks.

    When Westinghouse was attempting to build its share in the lightbulb
    market in the 1970s, it paid some accounts for their existing inventory of
    competitive bulbs.

    In a buy-out, the firm going after a new account pays the account's costs of
    switching. Thus A may pay the account's costs of (say) disposing of its
    inventory of B's products.

    What kind of a cost is the cost of a competitive buy-out?

5. Below is a pro forma operating statement for a Wendy's franchise as of
    1978. The figures given are for an annual sales volume of $400,000. The
    franchisee expects his volume to increase by $100,00 or $200,000 in the
    next year or so. Classify each of the costs in the statement as either
    variable, fixed, or programmed.

    Pro Forma Operating Statement for a Wendy's Franchise
    (as of 1978)
    (In thousands)

Sales	$400.0	100.0%
Cost of goods sold		
Manager	16.4	4.1
Co-manager	13.5	3.4
Assistant/trainee	17.4	4.4
Crew	40.0	10.0
Total labor	87.3	21.8
Food	156.0	39.0
Paper	13.6	3.4
Laundry	0.8	0.2
Total cost of goods sold	257.7	64.4
Gross profit	142.3	35.6

Pro Forma Operating Statement – continued

Operating expenses

Rent	33.0	8.3
Royalty	16.0	4.0
Insurance	3.4	0.9
Payroll taxes	8.2	2.0
Real estate taxes	2.5	0.6
Other taxes	1.2	0.3
Supplies and uniforms	6.4	1.6
Telephone and utilities	12.0	3.0
Repairs and maintenance	7.2	1.8
Trash removal	1.8	0.5
Advertising and promotion	16.0	4.0
Office expense	1.7	0.4
Miscellaneous	0.4	0.1
Depreciation	8.0	2.0
Total operating expenses	117.8	29.4
Operating profit before tax	24.6	6.1

Source: Robert L. Emerson, *Fast Food: The Endless Shakeout* (New York: Lebhar-Friedman, 1979), 153. Emerson got his figures from Wendy's.

6. The following costs are for a gasoline service station pumping eighty thousand gallons a month (as of the early 1980s). Rent is based on the replacement cost of the station. Which costs are likely to vary with changes in amount of gasoline pumped?

Item	*Monthly Cost*
Rent	$ 3,161
Electricity	350
Water	75
Gas	250
Maintenance	200
Insurance	150
Mortgage insurance	180
Shortages	100
Professional services	180
Waste removal	35
Supplies	150

Item	*Monthly Cost*
Licenses	50
Taxes	175
State vehicle tax	150
Credit card fees	2,240
Interest	75
Payroll	2,400
Uniforms	100
Telephone	75
Advertising	50
Total monthly costs	10,206

Source: U.S. Congress, Senate Committee on Small Business, *Current Petroleum Marketing Practices and Their Impact on Small Business* (97th Cong., 2nd sess., 1982).

7. A research and development (R&D) group is asked to engineer a special order for a customer. It estimates that the special work will cost $32,000. From the point of view of sales management, what kind of a cost is this?

8. "Marketing research expenditures are one of the first things cut when business sours."

    This seems to mean that marketing research is (typically) a programmed cost. Do you agree? Can you think of any realistic situations in which marketing research is likely to be a variable cost? or a fixed cost?

9. In the 1950s in Germany, television time was so scarce that advertisers had to buy time a year or more in advance. What kind of cost was the cost of TV advertising at the time?

10. Students often complain to the dean about my teaching. As part of their complaint, they often argue that my wretched teaching stings even more because the course is costing them some $1,700, which is the total tuition for one year divided by ten courses.

    What kind of a cost is that $1,700?

Questions on Sunk Costs

Most people from time to time fall prey to the sunk cost fallacy, that is, they allow sunk costs to influence their decisions. (It should be added they do this without mortal hurt.) To help the reader better understand sunk costs the following questions raise, or appear to raise, questions about what sunk costs are and how they should be analyzed.

1. In Book Fourteen of *The Iliad* the Greek king Agamemnon proposes in a weak moment that the Greeks forget the siege of Troy and sail home. Odysseus upbraids him saying, in part, that the Greeks have been fighting for nine years now. "Would you give up after all this time and sail back to Greece, taking your losses?" Is Odysseus using a sunk cost argument? Is he using it correctly? If not, just what is his argument?

2. You have just made it through to the end of the story in *War and Peace*, and to your dismay you discover there are still another hundred pages of Tolstoy's musings on history. You reason as follows:

   If I don't finish *War and Peace* now, I never will. Besides I've already read eleven hundred pages. All that time and effort will be wasted in a sense if I don't go on and finish, although I really loved what I read, great story, great characters. I *am* going to finish it, otherwise it will nag me, knowing that I never read the whole thing.

   What if anything does this have to do with sunk cost?

3. A car has just run over your friend's dog. In an unthinking moment, you try to comfort her by telling her that what's done is done, water over the dam, and other similar cliche's. She is not consoled. What does this tell you about the force of the sunk cost argument?

4. In the nineteenth century, British army officers were expected not to marry young. As one author has written, the rule was that "subalterns may not marry, captains might marry, majors should marry, and lieutenant-colonels must marry." Having reached suitable age and rank–say a major at age forty–some went about courting with business-like standards, fixing the amount they would spend on any one woman. "If, say, £100 was spent without results, they would cut their losses and begin anew."[1]

   What does "cut their losses" have to do with sunk cost? Just what does "cut their losses" mean?

5. A (lucky) speculator buys some stock for $40,000. When it increases in value to eighty thousand, he considers selling half of it for forty thousand. "If I do sell half," he says, "I will get back my original investment. Then I get a free ride on the rest of the stock. What should I do?"

   You do not know, of course. But you can address one issue: is sunk cost involved in any way? If so, how, and what is the correct analysis of the problem?

6. The university library has purchased only the first two volumes of a five-volume collection of the letters of some seventeenth-century German aesthete, say. When questioned by the head of the German department, the librarian says that she has very little money in her budget and can not purchase the rest. The professor objects, pointing out that while the first two volumes have some limited use, the full set would be much more useful. "Having already bought two we must protect our 'investment' and buy the other three." Is the professor committing the sunk cost fallacy, or arguing correctly, or both?

7. Many expenditures come in two parts. You pay to enter the Calcutta Zoo, then find you must pay a second time to see the white Bengal tigers; you pay to enter the natural history museum but must pay again to enter the planetarium; you pay tuition but must pay extra for lab fees in geology.

    Would it *ever* be correct for you to say (in essence), "I've paid once but I'm not going to pay a second time?" What does the answer tell you about the sunk cost principle?

8. By the early 1980s, the British had been trying for many years to transfer the Falkland Islands to Argentina through diplomatic means. Unfortunately the islanders did not wish to become Argentine.

    After the war in 1982, some gloomily wrote that now it was not possible for Britain to withdraw from the Falklands for at least a generation or more, because otherwise the loss of life would seem to the British public to have been in vain.

    Have such writers fallen for the sunk cost fallacy? Has the British public? Assuming that they writers are correct–as they most certainly are–what does this say about the force of the sunk cost argument? Just why is it that understanding and using the sunk cost principle is so difficult for so many?

9. Many people behave as if they disbelieve the sunk cost principle. That presumably is why we have so many folk sayings advising us to ignore sunk costs. That is, if people really believed that bygones were in fact bygones, these sayings would disappear.

    So while the microeconomist sees sunk cost as clearly irrelevant to decisions, most others do not. For them, at least some of the time, sunk costs appear to count.

    What implications, if any, does this have for your behavior as a manager?

10. "We must protect our investment" and "we have to get back that money that

we spent" usually indicate that the speaker is fallaciously arguing the relevance of sunk costs. Is the following an example?

The heart of the Kennedy family's fortune is the Merchandise Mart in Chicago, a huge building that Joseph Kennedy bought in 1945 for $1 million. When other Chicago real estate interests planned a new building that would lure tenants away, the Kennedys countered with a proposed Apparel Center that would cost some $45 million and tie Kennedy interests even more closely to the health of the Chicago real estate market. Their advisor, André Meyer, imperator of Lazard Frères, advised the Kennedys that although the required investment was large, "the investment was prudent and necessary to protect their existing investment."[2]

11. In 1969 Procter and Gamble introduced *Pringles,* a food product that is said to resemble potato chips. The brand never achieved what has been reported as P&G's objectives of $200 million a year in sales and a market share of 25 percent. (Its best year was 1975 when sales were 110 million, but that was after the sharp price increases in 1973 and 1974.) According to a story in *Business Week,* though, P&G was not about to give up:

> The company is apparently going to stay with *Pringles* because it has too much invested to back out now. ... [It had spend an estimated $50 million advertising *Pringles* and invested heavily in two chip making plants in Tennessee and North Carolina.] Although *Pringles* are causing a giant marketing headache, P&G is obviously reluctant to give up its toehold in the lucrative but highly competitive snack-food field. "Procter & Gamble is not going to walk away when it has such an investment tied up," says George Waydo, vice-president of marketing for Borden Inc.'s Wise/Old London Foods Division.[3]

On the surface this appears simply as yet another example of the sunk cost fallacy. Is it? Under what conditions would it be incorrect to conclude that the sunk cost fallacy is involved? That is, can you explain P&G's behavior in such a way as to show that it is not committing the sunk cost fallacy?

12. The *Wall Street Journal* ran a story on a patented AIDS treatment, DDC, manufactured by Hoffman-La Roche. The drug was being illegally copied by "the AIDS-treatment underground" to provide cheap access to the drug for AIDS patients. Hoffman-La Roche was not amused, according to the story. "Roche has spent five years developing the drug and is faced with recouping a huge investment ... millions of dollars."

"Recouping a huge investment" is just another instance of the press's misunderstanding sunk costs, right?

Questions on Opportunity Costs

1. A grandmother gives her teenage grandson a $15 gift certificate for a compact disc. The boy goes to the store, has a hard time choosing between two CDs, but finally picks one.

    What did the CD he chose cost him?

2. Fred Turner preferred to own land for McDonald's stores rather than lease. The chapter argued that Turner was wrong and that owning and leasing were the same.

    But are they? Leasing involves a cash outlay every year, owning involves none; and therefore owning is less risky in recessions or when business turns down. Turner was right after all, right?

3. When one parent stays home to care for young children, it is usually the mother, not the father. You can doubtless think of several reasons why such a division of family duties occurs. One of the reasons is based on opportunity cost.

    What is it?

Chapter 4

Problems In Marketing Arithmetic

1. The Melbourne (Australia) *Age* reported that a novice Hari Krishna member had stolen $985 worth of flowers from a wholesale florist. The story also reported the flowers had a retail value of $1,970. What is the retail gross margin for fresh flowers in Melbourne?

2. A manufacturer sells an item at factory for $26. Normal wholesale margins are about 20 percent and normal retail margins are about 50 percent. What will the retail price be?

3. (a) Given the following gross margins on price compute the markups on cost: 20 percent, 40 percent, 50 percent.

    (b) Given the following markups on cost, compute the gross margins as a percent of price: 25 percent, 33 1/3 percent, 50 percent.

4. An item carries a manufacturer's suggested retail price of $16.60. Retail margins run about 33 1/3 percent, wholesale margins about 7 percent. What

is the manufacturer's factory price?

5. A manufacturer's product usually sells at retail for $70. Typical retail margins are 43 percent, typical wholesale margins are 20 percent. The broker whom the manufacturer uses to contact wholesalers receives 3 percent of the factory price in commissions. What is the factory price?

6. A company sells 40 percent of its major product direct to industrial end users, who pay $6.40 a unit. The rest of the sales goes through trade channels to consumers, who also pay $6.40. The company uses a broker for these sales, who receives 4 percent of the factory price. Wholesalers normally get 8 percent and retailers 33 percent. The firm's salesmen who sell to industrial users receive a 30 percent commission. What is the average revenue at factory per unit sold?

7. A retailer had opening inventory at cost of $900,000 and closing inventory of $1,300,000. His average gross margin was 30 percent, and his turnover was 15. What were his sales at retail?

8. A wine retailer tells you that his standard markup is 50 percent, but that he gives a 15 percent discount on case purchases. What is his gross margin when a purchaser buys a case?

9. Standard terms of sale granted by toothpaste manufacturers to retailers are 2 percent 30 net 60. Toothpaste has a turnover at retail of nine or ten or eleven times a year. What do these facts imply for a retailer's working capital requirements?

10. Here are some typical sales and estimates of studio revenues for some top selling video tapes.

Title	Estimated Units Sold (in millions)	Studio Revenues (in millions)
Batman	13.0	$195
ET 12.5	187	
Bambi	10.5	168
Who Framed Roger Rabbit	8.5	119
Cinderella	7.5	124
Land Before Time	4.0	60
Top Gun	3.5	56
Lady and the Tramp	3.2	58
Crocodile Dundee	2.5	38

Source: *Forbes* (Feb. 5, 1990), 39.

A typical retail price was $20 a tape in video rental stores and $17 in mass merchandisers like K-Mart and in grocery stores and gasoline stations.

What are typical retail gross margins for these tapes in these two channels?

11. A short piece in a marketing newsletter urged readers to consider trading terms for price, that is, reducing terms from (say) net 30 to net 10 and lowering price. How much of a reduction in price would the change from thirty to ten days permit? Assume that money costs 15 percent.

12. A report on a textile company contained the following somewhat cryptic figures.

Width	Mill Net Style	Less Price	Wholesale Discount	Wholesale Percentage Price	Suggested Retail Markup	Retailer Price	Percentage Markup
54"	White & Colors	$0.74	0.6845	0.7860	12.8%	$1.29	39.1%

Thus, the mill net price of 54-inch wide, white and colored fabric is $0.74 a yard, the wholesale price is $0.786 a yard, and so on.

Can the headings be reconciled with the figures? Do it.

13. A retailer normally enjoys a 52 percent gross margin on fashionable women's suits. During a two-week promotion the suit maker reduces the wholesale price by 20 percent. At the same time the retail buyer cuts her normal price so as to yield a 48 percent gross margin instead of 52 percent.

How much is the retail price reduced during the sale?

14. At first glance it seems odd that gross margin is taken as a percentage of price instead of cost. Wouldn't it be more natural to think about markups on cost? A merchant buys a blouse for $90, marks it up $65, and sells it for $155. Why shouldn't the merchant think of the margin as a 72 percent markup on cost instead of a 42 percent margin on price?

There is a solid business reason why the merchant thinks of gross margin as a percent of price instead of cost. What is it?

Slightly More Difficult Problems

There are no difficult problems in marketing arithmetic.

Chapter 5 - Questions on Marginal Analysis

Elementary Problems

1. One of the examples in this chapter discusses the proportion of tenured faculty who are women. It says

   The only way–the *only* way–that the average can increase is for the marginal figure to be greater than the average.

   Why is it the only way?

2. Chapter 3 gave several folk sayings about sunk costs. But there were none in this chapter about the need to look at marginal values instead of average values. Can you think of any sayings that do urge the marginal point of view? Why do you think there are a number that deal with sunk cost and (apparently) none (or at most a few) that deal with marginalism?

3. The chapter says a checker in a supermarket can process a coupon in six or seven seconds, which is surely the right order of magnitude. Still something doesn't quite ring right about this example. What is it? and What does it mean?

Slightly More Difficult Problems

Advertising vacant apartments

Eight investors form a limited partnership buy a garden apartment in North San Diego County. Their first problem is to increase rental income. They know that their vacancy rate is somewhat higher than competing apartment houses but that their monthly rents are competitive. Perhaps they need to advertise, the traditional way of filling vacancies.

The partners found themselves in a dispute over how much to spend for advertising. One of the partners said:

   We should set a budget for our advertising. But what should it be? I guess we should spend as much on advertising as it is worth to fill the vacancy. But each of these apartments rents for about $11,000/year.

Does this mean that we should spend as a maximum about $10,000 to fill each apartment?

Another said:

That argument makes no sense at all. The apartment is only worth one month's rent, $900 right? So we should only spend *that* much. You agree? OK, then I say it's really worth *two* years rent–we normally get two-year leases–and that we should spend $22,000. Why set a budget? We have to keep on advertising until we get tenants. What would we do if we exceeded our budget? Stop advertising? And let the vacancy go on? Don't be ridiculous. This is only an $800,000-a-year business. We're no big firm, and we shouldn't strain to bring big firm methods–budgeting and all that–into what is essentially a two-bit operation.

What is the correct analysis? How much should be spent on filling a vacancy?

The UAW's proposal

Some years ago the leader of the United Auto Workers (UAW) suggested to a congressional committee that automobile manufacturers lower their prices by 4 percent. He wanted to stimulate the sale of new cars and thereby increase work for his members.

At the time a new car cost around $2,500. Published studies of the response of new car sales to price changes had shown that a price cut of 4 percent would increase the number of cars sold by about 6 percent. (That is, the price elasticity was -1.5.)

Here are the figures before the suggested price cut and after. Answer the questions that follow.

Before the price cut

	Totals* (millions)	Per Car
Revenues	$2,500	$2,500
Expenses		
Variable	$1,840	$1,840
Fixed	460	460
Total expenses	2,300	2,300
Profit before tax	200	200

* Assuming a volume of one million cars

After the price cut

	Totals** (millions)	Per Car
Revenues	$2,544	$2,400
Expenses		
Variable	$1,950	$1,840
Fixed	460	460
Total expenses	<u>2,410</u>	<u>2,300</u>
Profit before tax	134	100

** Assuming (1) a price elasticity of -1.5 and (2) a price reduction from $2,500 to $2,400 per car.

(a) Are the numbers in after-the-cut table correct? If yes, go on; if not, correct them and then go on.

(b) Note that after the price cut (1) more cars are sold and (2) each one sells at a price exceeding variable cost. How then can it be that profit before tax declines from $200 million to $134 million?

(c) "At the time a new car cost around $2,500." That must have been a long time ago. How long?

Cost of owning a car

The American Automobile Association (AAA) regularly estimates the average cost of owning a car. Recently the AAA produced estimates for a composite of three domestic cars, a subcompact Ford Escort, a mid-sized Ford Taurus, and a full-sized Chevy Caprice, driven 15,000 miles a year.

Typical figures ran between 35¢ and 40¢ a mile:

New England	38.8¢ a mile
Midwest	35.8¢ a mile
Mid-Atlantic and West	37.3¢ a mile

These figures are averages. Estimate as best you can the marginal cost of (say) driving another ten miles (or another hundred). What you want is not a precise figure but an order of magnitude. Are the average and the marginal about the same? If not, which is bigger and (roughly) by how much?

Chapter 6 - Problems In Marketing Control

Elementary Problems

1. Brand X is a consumer product with a retail price of $10. Retail gross margins on the product are 33 1/3 percent, while wholesalers take a 12 percent margin.

    Brand X and its direct competitors sell a total of 20 million units a year. Brand X has 24 percent of this market.

    Variable manufacturing costs (labor, materials, packaging) are $0.90/unit. Fixed manufacturing costs are $900,000. Factory overhead for the brand, allocated at 210 percent of direct labor, is $2,720,000 at current production levels.

    The production of Brand X uses plant and equipment with a current book value after depreciation of $1.4 million, although if production were discontinued the salvage value of plant and equipment would be somewhere between $200,000 and $400,000.

    The advertising budget for the brand is $2.4 million a year. The product manager's salary and expenses for his office total $350,000 a year. Salesmen were paid a 10 percent commission. Shipping costs, breakage, and the like, are $0.20/unit.

    (a) Prepare a marketing control statement for Brand X.

    (b) What is the unit gross marketing contribution?

    (c) What must the brand sales be to just cover programmed marketing expenses?

    (d) What market share does the brand need to break even? What is the value of a share point?

    Industry demand is expected to increase by 15 percent next year. The product manager is considering raising his advertising budget to $5 million.

    (e) If the advertising budget is raised, how many units will the brand have to sell to break even?

    (f) How many units will the brand have to sell to achieve the same net marketing contribution as this year?

(g) What will the market share have to be next year for the net marketing contribution to be the same as this year?

(h) What market share does the brand need to have a net marketing contribution of $21 million?

2. Return to the Pro Forma Operating Statement for Wendy's (in the questions at the end of those for Chapter 3). Prepare a marketing control statement from the figures.

3. Banks make a bundle from credit cards. To see why, assemble the following into a marketing control statement.

Number of cards	5.1 million
Annual fee per card	$15
Average balance per card	$1,300
Average annual interest rate	18.9%
Merchant discount[1]	2.6%
Average monthly billings per card	$1,166
Cost of money[2]	8%
Bad debts (% of outstanding balances)	3.6%
Advertising	$23 million
Sales force costs[3]	$43 million
All other costs	$6.7 million

Notes

1. Merchants pay for the privilege of accepting your card. When you charge, say $100 purchase, the merchant deposits your charge slip in his bank. But he does not get the full $100. He gets $100 less 2.6 percent or $97.40.

2. In simple terms, banks borrow in the money market at 8 percent and relend it to credit card customers at 18.9 percent.

3. The sales force calls on merchants, restaurants, corporate users, and the like.

4. PDQ Systems, in Aspen, Colorado, sells 75,000 laser jet printers per year, which gives it a market share of 11 percent. PDQ offers its retailers and wholesalers a combined margin of 35 percent on a retail price of $2,000 per unit.

Beall Compson, the president, says that variable production costs amount to

$775 per unit and fixed manufacturing costs total $12,750,000 per year. In addition, shipping and packaging costs of $50 per unit must be paid by PDQ. G&A costs are $11.4 million and the annual advertising budget is $1.95 million. PDQ's forty-man sales force plus sales management costs $4.3 million a year.

(a) What are PDQ Systems' fixed costs?

(b) What are PDQ's variable costs per unit?

(c) What is the unit contribution?

(d) What is the break-even volume for PDQ (units)?

(e) What market share is needed to achieve this volume?

(f) What are PDQ's current profits?

(g) Compson expects to sell 1 to 2 percent more printers if he raises his ad budget by 20 percent. Should he raise his budget?

(h) What would be the break-even level (in units) if the advertising budget were raised?

(i) As an extra inducement, along with the extra advertising, Compson is considering offering two free font cartridges with every printer sold. The cartridges cost $87.50 each. Now what is the analysis?

Slightly More Difficult Problems

New York State Lottery

When it began in 1968, the New York State Lottery gave its licensed retail sales agents a retail gross margin of 5 percent. The lottery law required the Lottery Commission to pay out 30 percent of gross receipts at retail in prizes. First year sales were just over $60 million, whereas sales of $360 million had been expected (see figures below.) One of the earliest proposals for hyping the lottery's poor sales was to increase this gross margin from 5 to 7 percent or from 5 to 10 percent.

How much would sales have to increase for the lottery to be just as well off after these increases as before?

New York State
Pro Forma Income Statement
1968-69

		(millions)
Gross receipts		$360
Expenses		
Commissions	$18	
Administration	36	
Prizes	<u>108</u>	<u>162</u>
Net receipts		198

Life Cereal

In 1961, Life cereal, produced by the Quaker Oats Company, sold to retailers for $5.60 per case of twenty-four ten-ounce boxes. Retail gross margins typically ran 15 to 20 percent, and the typical retail price was about 30¢. At the end of 1961, Life had a 1.4 percent share of weight of the ready-to-eat (RTE) market. Sales at factory were about $2.7 million in 1961.

The cost structure for cereals looked like this:

Net sales		100.0%
Manufacturing		
Fixed	12.9	
Variable	9.6	
Distribution and delivery	<u>5.4</u>	57.9
Marketing		
Advertising	15.0	
Sales price	3.5	
Market research	<u>0.5</u>	19.0
Administrative and general		<u>4.0</u>
Total costs (above)		80.9%
Available for merchandising, and other costs and profit		19.1%

Source: National Commission on Food Marketing, 1966 Study.

Manufacturers of RTE cereals typically maintained an advertising-to-sale (A/S) ratio of 15 percent to support their brands; but Life's A/S ratio was somewhat lower (about 8 percent) because of difficulties in finding effective copy themes. Hence Life's advertising was about 8 percent of $2.7 million = $220,000.

In 1961, Life's brand manager was considering an increase in advertising from the current budget to $345,000 plus a one-time test of a sampling scheme estimated to cost $135,000 (in which free samples of Life would be given away, or "sampled").

Prepare a marketing control statement for Life. Use it (and any other relevant information) to evaluate the proposal.

Hot Dog Man

One member of the Wall Street establishment is Louie Stathopoulos, a thirty-year-old hot dog vendor who works on Broadway just north of Exchange Place.[4] As best you can, prepare Louie's marketing control statement from the following information. What conclusion do you draw?

As one might expect from his proximity to Wall Street, Louie works banker's hours, 10 in the morning to 3:30 in the afternoon (although he leaves his house at 6 A.M. and usually gets back around 9 P.M.). He does most of his business in the summer. Business drops in half during the winter.

He sells between 100 and 150 hot dogs and seventy-five sodas a day. The hot dogs go for $1, the sodas for $0.75. He also sells twenty knishes at $0.75 each and ten smoked sausages at $1 each. His hot dog cart has a grill heated by propane gas. It costs between $4,000 and $5,000 new and lasts about five years. One time a truck backed into it and it cost $1,000 to get it repaired. He pays $275 a month to garage his cart.

A pound of hot dogs, about seven dogs, costs $2.50. Knishes are thirty for $9.75, sausages six for $2.35, and sodas $8 for a case of twenty-four.

Insurance premiums run $500 a year. He needs fifteen pounds of propane a week at $12. Every day he uses one hundred straws, a gallon of onions, a sixteen-ounce bottle of ketchup, half a gallon of mustard, six hundred napkins, and $40 worth of ice. "People get one hot dog, but they want five or six napkins. This city is hung up on napkins."

Fines for obstructing crosswalks, subway entrances, and fire hydrants start at $10, but the fourth fine in a two-year period is $1,000. Louie has gotten stung a couple of times for $1,000. In 1987, when he parked too near a city park, city officials seized his cart. It took him a month to get it back.

Like all Wall Streeters (and many hot dog men), Louie has plans. He saves money that he uses to buy additional carts that he staffs with hired help. In 1987 he had five others that worked the financial district. Generally each of his hot dog men got $40 a day and a split of the profits beyond $40.

Testing Price

A retailer of expensive cookware sells through its retail stores and a large catalog operation. It recently tested an imported, upscale food processor at four prices in its fall catalog. The variable cost before customs and related costs was $151.30. Customs and related added another 5 percent to the cost, and the retailer added another 13.5 percent to cover overhead. The catalog mailing involved a run of 1,830,000 pieces, at a cost of $85 per thousand, exclusive of postage. Thirty-two thousand of the catalogs displayed the food processor, 8,000 at each of the four prices. Early results of the test were compiled five weeks after the catalog drop, as follows:

Price	$359	$329	$299	$269
Units sold*	107	213	201	418

* before returns

What should the retailer do next?

Video Tapes

Early in the 1980s, movie studios started selling video tapes of their movies. They usually carried a list price of $89.95, which gave the retailer a gross margin of 28 percent. Sales ran to several hundred thousand, the chief buyers being video rental stores who bought the tapes and rented them at $2 or $3 or $4 a night.

By the end of the decade, the movie studios had realized that at least on some videos they might be able to net more income if they set wholesale prices around $15.50. At these lower prices the best selling tapes sold several million copies. Show, if you can, that the studios were right to change from skim to penetration pricing.

Direct Mail Promotion

Below is a form typical of those used by direct mail houses to explore proposals. Redo the figures to get a proper marketing control statement.

Worksheet for Direct Mail Project

Selling price | 35.40 |

Service charge | 3.50 |

I.   **Total revenue** | 38.90 |

II. **Cost of filling the order**

a.   Merchandise | 14.35 |

b.   Royalties @ 1.5% | .22 |

c.   Order processing and shipping | 2.30 |

d.   United Parcel | 2.25 |

e.   Premium included with product | |

f.   Local or state taxes @ 1.75% | .25 |

g.   Overhead @ 14.5% | 2.08 |

Total cost of filling the order | 21.45 |

III. **Estimated returns,**
     cancellations or refunds | 8.2 % |

IV. **Returns expenses**

a.   Postage and handling | 2.46 |

b.   Cleaning returns | 1.13 |

Total cost of handling returns | 3.59 |

V.   **Expected returns cost (III x**
          Total cost of handling returns) | .29 |

VI.   **Estimated proportion bad debts** | 1.093 % |

VII.   **Expected bad debt costs (I x VI)** | .43 |

VIII.   **Total variable order costs** | 22.17 |

IX. **Return factor (100 - III)** | 91.8 % |

X.   **Direct order cost (VIII x IX)** | 20.35 |

XI. **Unit profit per order (I - X)** | 18.55 |

XII. **Returned merchandise credit (III x IIa)** | 1.18 |

XIII. **Net profit per order (XI + XII)** | 19.73 |

Silvermark Products, Inc.

Silvermark Products (SP) manufactures small appliances and cookware—irons, blow driers, coffee makers, small vacuum cleaners, and the like. One of its leading lines is kitchen mixers. The mixer market is highly competitive, mature, and growing at only 3.5 percent per year except the Deluxe model, which was not expected to increase at all in the next year.

The present SP line consists of three models that are sold direct to retailers: the Deluxe, the Standard, and the Economy.

	Factory Selling Price	Variable Cost per Unit	Monthly Sales, (Units)
Deluxe	$125.00	$47.00	3,000
Standard	70.00	30.00	11,000
Economy	45.00	22.00	17,000

The sales is an average over the most recent year. Sales peak sharply in December; they exhibit a lesser peak in June. Retailers usually took a 25 percent gross margin before sales promotion allowances. Programmed sales costs were expected to be $500,000 in the coming year.

SP has recently been approached by a major department store chain (with stores mostly on the West Coast and Southeast) to manufacture a private brand under its GetMor label for next year. The private brand would be produced in SP's Alabama factory, which was expected to have excess capacity for the next eighteen to twenty-four months. The proposed contract would be for three years with an option to extend for two more. But it could be cancelled on three month's notice prior to the end of each year of the contract.

The chain wanted two models. The GetMor would be similar to the Economy model, and the GetMor Plus would be virtually identical to the Standard model. In order to produce these brands, SP would have to spend $55,000 on tooling for appearance trim. Relevant sales and estimated cost data were as follows:

	Factory Selling Price	Variable Cost	Sales Forecast, Units per month
GetMor	$36.00	$18.00	8,000
GetMor Plus	55.00	26.00	3,500

Silvermark executives estimated that the chain would take an initial gross margin of around 35 percent. The sales forecast was for planning purposes only, as monthly volume would vary. If the two private brands were introduced, SP executives estimated that the GetMor would cannibalize 20 percent of the Economy line sales and the GetMor Plus would cannibalize 25 percent of the Standard line sales. SP had been told by corporate management that the plant would have to increase its gross marketing contribution of 10 percent if private brands were introduced.

Should SP accept the proposal? Why or why not?

Chapter 7

Elementary Problems

1. During a six-week promotion, a retail buyer of women's moderate-priced sportswear expects her retail gross margin per item to drop from $55 to $41.80. She normally sells about 160 items a month.

    How much must her unit sales increase to leave her no worse off?

2. A chain of shoe stores is considering opening yet another outlet, a decision that it makes several times a year. Given the figures below, how many pairs of shoes must be sold for the new store to be profitable?

	Per Pair	
Retail price	$ 78.00	100%
Cost of goods	50.70	65
Commission	3.90	5
Gross margin	23.40	30

Annual expenses:	
Salaries	$440,000
Advertising	176,000
Rent*	50,000
All other	44,000
	710,000

    * Rent is $50,000 plus 8 percent of gross sales.

3. For several years AB Plastics (ABP) has been the world's only supplier of a high-polymer resin that it sells for $0.75 a pound. A competitor has now developed a somewhat superior product. ABP thinks it can hold price at $0.75 for at least eighteen more months without serious erosion of share.

But it is also considering reducing prices between $0.06 and $0.12 to offset the competitor's superiority. Current variable costs run $0.083 per pound, and the plant and marketing costs that the product must cover run $13.47 million a year.

Evaluate the options of reducing price by $0.06 and by $0.12.

4. You read in a magazine that a chain of computer retailers is expanding. Overhead runs about $435,000 a year, and break-even sales volume is $2.4 million a year. What can you deduce?

Slightly More Difficult Problems

District of Columbia Lottery

The D.C. Lottery got off to a shaky start in its first years. Sales were $54,071,000, prizes $26,858,000, and contract services (paid to outside lottery supplies as a flat percentage of lottery revenues) were $9,863,000.

		(000)
Gross receipts		$54,071
Agents' fees		3,388
Net receipts		50,683
Costs		
Prizes	$26,858	
Contract services	9,863	
Overhead	16,471	53,192
Surplus		(2,509)

Among the suggestions made to improve its sales was that the lottery increase the fee given to retailers who sold lottery tickets from 6.3 percent of the ticket price to 10 percent. If this suggestion is adopted, how much must sales increase to just pay for higher commission?

Cosmair

Cosmair, Inc., is the U.S. licensed agent and distributor for L'Oreal, the French cosmetics firm with the third largest selling cosmetics line in the United States (Avon Products is first and Revlon second). The total U.S. cosmetics and fragrance industry had estimated sales of $7 billion in 1986. Cosmair's sales were broken down as follows: hair care products 34 percent, fragrances 33 percent, makeup 25 percent and skin care 8 percent. Three fragrances—Lancome,

Vanderbilt, and Polo–and L'Oreal hair coloring products accounted for 45 percent of sales, or $310 million. These products were seen by industry observers as cash cows that Cosmair was using to finance its aggressive growth in the U.S. market. Cosmair's advertising and promotional budget was expected to run around $230 million (in 1986).

In the spring of 1986 corporate management in New York City was considering a special $1.6 million addition to the advertising already scheduled for the southeast sales district #17, which comprised most of central and southern Florida.

District sales managers were responsible for generating product margin and for paying district operating, sales, and local marketing expenses from the product margin. What was left, called the district net, was the district's contribution to corporate headquarters.

Although district #17's sales had shown rapid growth in recent years, marketing managers in New York wanted to know whether extra advertising above the national advertising, would pay for itself. The tentative media buy was 60 percent in regional women's and fashion books and 40 percent in prime-time, spot television that delivered middle-income and upscale women.

The most recent sales forecast without the extra $1.6 million in advertising was for $10.85 million in 1986. Under newly introduced accounting rules based on a $400,000 study by Touche-Ross, each Cosmair sales district was charged with product costs as follows: labor, 14.7 percent of sales; materials, 30.1 percent; and product overhead at 50 percent of the direct labor rate. Sales people were paid between 2.5 percent and 4.5 percent of sales. In addition, there was a group sales bonus of 1/2 of 1 percent when sales were less than $13 million and 3 percent when sales were greater than $13 million.

What must sales be to just cover the extra $1.6 million in advertising?

No Hassle Treatment of Complaints

The complaints department handles roughly 1,000 complaints a month that involve refunds or credits to customers. The average investigation runs $45. A small proportion of the complaints must be investigated in the field by a service man. A far larger portion are examined (or tested) in the shop to determine the cause of the problem, and if possible, who caused it. Approximately 5 percent of claims are refused because the investigation turns up evidence of neglect or misuse by the customer. The average payment over the last six months was $135 per complaint.

The departmental expense is up, and management asks the complaints manager to cut the expenses. She proposes doing away with the investigation entirely and simply giving refunds and credits to all customers.

How much will the department save if the manager drops the investigation of complaints?

Notes

1   Byron Farwell, *For Queen and Country* (London: Allen Lane, 1981), 233-235.
2   Cary Reich, *Financier: the Biography of André Meyer* (New York: Morrow, 1983), 256.
3   *Business Week* (June 19, 1978), 30.
4   N. R. Kleinfield, "Selling the Sidewalk Frank," *New York Times* (July 26, 1987), Section 3, 4.

ANSWERS TO THE PROBLEMS

Chapter 2 - The Nature of Economic Theory

1. There is no final, indisputable answer to this question. Of course, the answer to the question depends on what one means by valuable. There are lots of valuable things that don't pass the test, like a child's love for his parents and most performing arts, say the opera or ballet. And there are things without value that seem to pay very well–fortune telling, perhaps, or, dare it be said, elaborate economic models of the economy.

    Does microeconomics pass the test of the market? Probably not. Microeconomists are not all that much richer than you or I, nor do microeconomists in colleges and universities feel comfortable about letting students choose freely. It is much easier to make microeconomics a required course.

2. They might reply as follows:

    (a) The argument is nothing more than a variant of the vulgar, anti-intellectual sneer–If you're so smart why ain't you rich? (But this reply does not answer the objection.)

    (b) Microeconomics is not prescriptive but normative, therefore it doesn't apply to me.

    (c) Microeconomics deals with behavior of the mass not of an individual, therefore it doesn't apply to me.

Chapter 3 - What a Marketer Needs to Know About Costs

General Questions on Costs

1. It's rough, but it does catch a good deal of the difference between the two. What the summary doesn't catch at all is the in-between programmed cost.

2. *Costs fixed in the short run* is a more accurate phrase. But the emphasis on the short run is too narrow. As the chapter illustrates, whether costs are fixed or variable depends on the nature of the control system and the nature of the decision. Thus my mortgage is a fixed cost until the decision arises whether I should sell my house and move in with my parents.

3. I am clearly better off. When I bought the £1,000 it cost me $1,100. But today it would cost $2,000. So I bought pound sterling for $1,100 that is now worth $2,000. At the same time it is true that the trip will cost me more. There is an implied alternative, not going. If I don't go, I can sell the pounds for $2,000. This is the opportunity cost of the trip and it will vary with the exchange rate.

   But the question suggests that this is not a possible alternative: "I *am* going. I *will* spend the money." When there are no alternatives, there are no opportunity costs. If I must go then the cost is zero–the $1,100 is sunk and not germane to my decision, and there are no alternative uses for the £1,000.

Questions on Cost Classifications

1. The costs incurred by the station are trivial. PSAs are usually run at off-peak times like the early morning and the summer. A PSA is usually not scheduled until the day before when the traffic department finds (say) an unsold thirty-second spot in the late afternoon and decides to fill the spot with a PSA.

   Some PSAs are scheduled. Then there is a cost, an opportunity cost of foregone revenue (if in fact the PSA runs in a time slot when a paid ad could have run).

   The question is an interesting one. To answer it the student has to know a bit about how radio and television stations schedule ads. For a fuller discussion see my book, *Marketing for Non-Profit Organizations* published by Auburn House.

2. Almost certainly it is a programmed cost, a kind of one-time, start-up cost that is a cost of getting into the remanufacturing business.

3. The cost of longer terms is primarily a programmed cost. IBM probably set a budget for the cash cost of the delayed payment terms. Of course, the cost will vary with the number of dealers taking up the offer, and the number of PC Jr's they buy.

4. The money lost on the initial sales is a cost of getting into the business. After a few months or so, the expense will disappear. It is not fixed, nor is it variable. It is probably a programmed cost.

5. *Wendy's*

    Whether the following classifications are right or not is of far less importance than thinking the issues through.

Cost of Goods Sold	*Type of Cost*
Manager	Probably fixed. It is hard to believe that someone getting $16,400 a year will also get a bonus, although he may.
Co-manager	Fixed–for the same reasons above.
Assistant trainee	Fixed. A trainee would never get a compensation based on sales.
Crew	Variable. This should vary as volume does. The franchisee will use part-time and half-time workers to adjust crew to sales. (In 1978, all crew members were paid $2.65 an hour, the minimum wage.)
Food	Variable. (It turns out that meat is 50 to 55 percent of the food bill.)
Paper	Variable.
Laundry	Variable. Varies with crew size (or it should), which varies with sales.

Operating expenses

Rent	Fixed.
Royalty	Variable. This is the royalty paid to Wendy's. Typically it is a percentage of sales. Note that the figure is exactly 4 percent (to two significant places), so you can guess that the royalty is 4 percent of sales.
Insurance	Fixed. Does this increase with volume? Probably not.
Payroll taxes	Variable. Varies with crew size, which varies with sales.
Real estate taxes	Fixed.
Other taxes	Fixed, probably.
Supplies and uniforms	Variable. Should vary with sales.
Telephone and utilities	Variable, but probably only a bit.
Repairs and maintenance	The more business the more need for repairs and maintenance. But these costs are not driven by sales. Repairs and maintenance can be postponed. So this is a programmed cost in the short run, and a variable cost in the long run.
Trash removal	Semi-variable? The garbage hauler probably charges by the dumpster, so no increase until the current dumpster is full.
Advertising and promotion	If this is local advertising, it is clearly a programmed cost. But the franchisee may estimate his sales and using an advertising-to-sale ratio and work backward, in which case advertising would increase each

	quarter (say) as sales increased. But even then it would not be variable cost.
	But there is a second possibility. This may be a fee paid to Wendy's. If so, it is like royalties, and is variable. It turns out this is right, and the previous paragraph is wrong.
Office expense	Fixed, except that an increase in sales from \$400,000 to \$500,000 or \$600,000 is a healthy increase and may require more office expense. So it may be semi-variable.
Miscellaneous	Fixed, because I don't know what these costs are.
Depreciation	Fixed, clearly fixed in the short run.

On the next page is the pro forma statement at four levels of sales. Check your answers against the figures given.

6.   All this takes is some guessing based on common sense.

Costs that clearly vary with gallonage
Electricity (to run the pumps)   Supplies
Credit card fees

Costs that clearly don't vary with gallonage

Rent	Waste removal
Maintenance	State vehicle tax
Professional services	Uniforms
Taxes	Gas
Payroll	Mortgage insurance
Advertising	Licenses
Water	Telephone
Insurance	

7.   The cost of the special work is a programmed cost. It certainly isn't variable; it certainly isn't fixed.

Pro Forma Operating Statement for a Wendy's Franchise (as of 1978)
(In thousands of dollars)

Sales	$400.0	100.0%	$500.0	100.0%	$600.0	100.0%	$700.0	100.0%
Cost of goods sold								
Manager	16.4	4.1	16.4	3.3	16.4	2.7	16.4	2.3
Co-manager	13.5	3.4	13.5	2.7	13.5	2.3	13.5	1.9
Assistant/trainee	17.4	4.4	17.4	3.5	17.4	2.9	17.4	2.5
Crew	40.0	10.0	49.4	9.9	60.6	10.1	70.4	10.1
Total labor	87.3	21.8	96.7	19.3	107.9	18.0	117.7	16.8
Food	156.0	39.0	195.0	39.0	232.8	38.8	267.4	38.2
Paper	13.6	3.4	17.5	3.5	22.2	3.7	25.9	3.7
Laundry	0.8	0.2	1.0	0.2	1.2	0.2	1.4	0.2
Total cost of goods sold	257.7	64.4	310.2	62.0	364.1	60.7	412.4	58.9
Gross profit	142.3	35.6	189.8	38.0	235.9	39.3	287.6	41.1
Operating expenses								
Rent	33.0	8.3	33.0	6.6	33.0	5.5	35.0	5.0
Royalty	16.0	4.0	20.0	4.0	24.0	4.0	28.0	4.0
Insurance	3.4	0.9	3.6	0.7	3.8	0.6	4.0	0.6
Payroll taxes	8.2	2.0	9.1	1.8	10.1	1.7	11.0	1.6
Real estate taxes	2.5	0.6	2.5	0.5	2.5	0.4	2.5	0.4
Other taxes	1.2	0.3	1.2	0.2	1.2	0.2	1.2	0.2
Supplies and uniforms	6.4	1.6	8.0	1.6	9.6	1.6	11.2	1.6
Telephone and utilities	12.0	3.0	14.5	2.9	16.8	2.8	18.9	2.7
Repairs and maintenance	7.2	1.8	9.5	1.9	12.0	2.0	14.7	2.1
Trash removal	1.8	0.5	1.8	0.4	1.8	0.3	1.8	0.3
Advertising and promotion	16.0	4.0	20.0	4.0	24.0	4.0	28.0	4.0
Office expense	1.7	0.4	1.7	0.3	1.7	0.3	1.7	0.2
Miscellaneous	0.4	0.1	0.5	0.1	0.6	0.1	0.7	0.1
Depreciation	8.0	2.0	8.0	1.6	8.0	1.3	8.0	1.1
Total operating expenses	117.8	29.4	133.4	26.7	149.1	24.9	166.7	23.8
Operating profit before tax	24.6	6.1	56.5	11.3	86.8	14.5	120.9	17.3

Source: Emerson, Robert L., *Fastfood: The Endless Shakeout*, (New York, Lebhar-Friedman: 1979), p. 153. Emerson got his figures from Wendy's.

8. Marketing research is indeed a programmed cost. I can think of only one situation in which marketing research might be fixed or variable and that is when a government contract specifies that the contractor spend a specified amount on marketing research—either a flat fee or an amount that varies with something.

    If marketing research were committed over a two- or three-year time horizon, it would be a fixed cost (by most lights). But I've never heard of research being bought this way.

9. Most people would say that it was fixed because (1) it presumably couldn't be changed and (2) the commitment was a long-term one, longer than a year. You might argue that it was programmed because it arose from a management decision. But all fixed costs are programmed in this sense. No—the best answer is that it was a fixed cost.

10. The $1,700 is some kind of average cost, that's obvious. But that's all it is. It is not a variable cost because students buy a year's education for their tuition. That is, they don't buy by the course. Before they pay it, tuition is a direct, avoidable, programmed cost. Afterward, once we get them in the MBA program and it is too late, tuition is a sunk cost.

    So the $1,700 is an average sunk cost. As such it serves no purpose that I can think of except as a rhetorical trick to gull one's opponents.

Answers to Questions on Sunk Costs

1. Odysseus is indeed arguing the relevance of sunk costs. All shrewd politicians do likewise.

2. It has nothing to do with "all that time and effort." If you can make still more time for Tolstoy's musing on history, read them. Otherwise, get on with your life.

3. The sunk cost argument is based on abstraction, which means the microeconomist views the death of your friend's dog and the death of a pit bull that has just ripped the arm off a defenseless child as the same. A sunk cost is a sunk cost is a sunk cost, as Gertrude Stein would have said if she had been a microeconomist.

    Conclusion: the sunk cost argument often fails to persuade, and rarely convinces.

4. To cut your losses does not mean to cut your losses. It means to take steps

so that your losses don't increase; it means to spend no more in unprofitable activities.

But this is precisely what the sunk cost principle focuses on, the difference between the past, which can never be changed, and the future, which is still (partially) under your control. So cutting your losses is another way of stating the sunk cost principle.

5. Sunk cost has nothing to do with this issue. The key cost is opportunity cost–what else could be done with the eighty thousand–now half in the stock, half in some other form.

6. The professor is indeed arguing the relevance of sunk costs, and his argument may well persuade the librarian.

7. Yes, it would be correct in some circumstances.

    (a) You pay to enter and then find you are short of money.

    (b) You pay to enter but judge the value of the next admission isn't worth the cost.

    Certainly what you have already paid shouldn't influence your decision, if you believe in the sunk cost principle.

8. The argument the writers are using is fallacious and correct. It is fallacious because it violates the sunk cost principle. It is correct because most British voters would agree that loss of life–a sunk cost surely–has much bearing on the Falklands question.

    Why is it so hard for people to understand and use the sunk cost principle? Probably because the evidence supporting the principle is weak. That is, those few who scrupulously adhere to the principle would be hard pressed to show that their decisions are any the better than decisions made by people who have never heard of it.

9. The implications are spelled out in the section of the chapter titled *How to Use Sunk Costs*. Ignore this inestimable advice at your peril.

10. Yes, it is an example of the sunk cost fallacy.

11. It may be an instance of the sunk cost fallacy, in which pride and the fear of admitting a mistake drove P&G to remain in a business that with hindsight it should have avoided. But it may not be an instance. The numbers may in fact look better than they did in 1969. Then, P&G had all the investment in

plant and advertising ahead of it. Now these are mostly behind it, and as a result *Pringles* may look better than ever. (Whether they taste better is a matter for another book.)

12. Wrong.

What the story presumably deals with is what Hoffmann-La Roche will do, now and in the future, as a result of the illegal copying. The investment is clearly sunk. But in planning the investment Hoffmann-La Roche estimated both (1) cash expenditures for development of the drug and for plant and equipment and (2) cash revenues. The revenues are now under attack as "thousands of patients–often with their doctors' blessing[s]" take the illegal copy.

What prompts Hoffmann-La Roche's actions then are not sunk costs but future revenues.

Answers to Questions on Opportunity Costs

1. The cost of the CD he buys is not $15. It is what he has to give up, which in this case is the other CD. The cost of the CD, that is, is the other CD.

2. No. Leasing involves a cash outlay. Owning does too–but it is cash foregone.

3. Women earn roughly two-thirds what men earn. Thus, if the mother stays home, the income foregone is less than if the father stays home. That is, the opportunity cost of the mother's time is lower. In plain English, it is cheaper if the mother stays home.

Chapter 4 - Elements of Marketing Arithmetic

Problems in Marketing Arithmetic

1.
Retail value	$1,970	100%
Wholesale value of flowers	985	50
Gross margin	985	50

Fifty percent is a typical gross margin for a florist.

2. Somewhere around $65, because $26/(0.5)(0.8) = $65. That is, working backward,

Retail price	$65.00	100%	
Retail gross margin	32.50	50	
Wholesale price	32.50	50	100%
Wholesale gross margin	6.50		20
Factory price	26.00		80

3. Reason the answers to this one from first principles. Take a 20 percent gross margin on price. If the price is $10, the markup is $2, and the cost must be $8. Hence the markup on cost is $2/$8 or 25 percent.

    (a) 25 percent, 66 2/3 percent, 100 percent.

    (b) 20 percent, 25 percent, 33 1/3 percent.

4. | Retail price | $ 16.60 | 100% | |
    |---|---|---|---|
    | Retail gross margin | 5.53 | 33 1/3 | |
    | Wholesale price | 11.07 | 66 2/3 | 100% |
    | Wholesale gross margin | 0.77 | | 7 |
    | Factory price | 10.30 | | 93 |

5. | Retail price | $70.00 | 100% | |
    |---|---|---|---|
    | Retail gross margin | 30.10 | 43 | |
    | Wholesale price | 39.90 | 57 | 100% |
    | Wholesale gross margin | 7.98 | | 20 |
    | Factory price | 31.92 | | 80 |

6. There are two ways in which product reaches customers.

    (a) Direct to end users

		Per unit
Price	$ 6.40	100%
Commission	1.92	30
Revenue from direct sales	4.48	70

    (b) Through trade channels

Retail price	$ 6.40	100%	
Retail gross margin	2.11	33	
Wholesale price	4.29	67	100%
Wholesale gross margin	0.34		8
Factory price	3.95		92	100
Broker's commission	0.16			4
Revenue from channel sales	3.79			96

    Since 40 percent goes direct at $4.48 per unit and 60 percent goes through channels at \$3.79 per unit, the (rounded) average revenue per unit is

$$
\begin{array}{rcl}
\$\ 4.48 \times 0.4 & = & \$1.79 \\
3.79 \times 0.6 & = & \underline{2.27} \\
& & \$4.06
\end{array}
$$

The lengthy calculation for the trade channels can be abbreviated:

$$
\begin{array}{l}
6.40 \times (1 - 0.33) \times (1 - 0.08) \times (1 - 0.04) \\
6.40 \times \quad 0.67 \quad \times \quad 0.92 \quad \times \quad 0.96 \quad = \$3.79
\end{array}
$$

7. *Average inventory*

At cost $1/2(900 + 1,300) = 1,100$ (that is, \$1.1 million)

At retail $1,100/0.7 = 1,570$ (that is, \$1.57 million)

Because the (average) inventory turns 15 times a year, sales must be \$1.57 million x 15 = \$24 million a year.

8. The question says that his markup is 50 percent. That probably means markup on cost, not gross margin, for two reasons: (1) in common use, the word "markup" usually means a cost-plus percentage, (2) a 50 percent markup on cost is a 33 percent gross margin on retail price, which is the correct order of magnitude for wine (at least more correct than a 50 percent gross margin). Pick a basis and proceed from there. Let cost be \$100.

	Normal *Gross Margin*		*Case* *Gross Margin*	
Price	\$ 150	100%	\$ 127.50*	100%
Cost	100	67	100.00	88
Gross margin	50	33	27.50	22

* \$150 less 15% is \$127.50

9. If he pays in sixty days, the retailer will have sold the stock before he has to pay for it. Hence he need not invest any working capital in toothpaste. If he pays in thirty days, he will have sold most of the stock and will have very little working capital invested.

Turnover	Days to Turn Stock	Required Working Capital Investment, Days Over 30
9	41	11
10	36	6
11	33	3

Thus, if his stock turns ten times a year and he pays in thirty days, his working capital investment is six days worth of toothpaste sales (at cost).

10. Divide studio revenues by units to get an estimate of the wholesale price.

Title	Estimated Units Sold (in millions)	Wholesale Studio Revenues (in millions)	Price
Batman	13.0	$195	$15.00
ET 12.5	187	14.96	
Bambi	10.5	168	16.00
Who Framed Roger Rabbit	8.5	119	14.00
Cinderella	7.5	124	16.53
Land Before Time	4.0	60	15.00
Top Gun	3.5	56	16.00
Lady and the Tramp	3.2	58	18.13
Crocodile Dundee	2.5	38	15.20
Average			$15.65

So at $20, a representative gross margin (GM) would be (20 - 15.65)/20 = 21.8 percent. The question says prices were below $20, so the gross margin is below 22 percent. Mass merchants who sold at $17 are getting GMs of 7.9 percent. The president of the video dealers trade association was quoted as saying that competition was forcing him to sell at eleven cents above cost, an implied margin of 7/10 of 1 percent. (But anyone who believes the video business is _this_ bad shouldn't be allowed to dress himself.)

11. The correct way to do this problem is to use discounted cash flow. But over a twenty-day period you can fake it. Say the product costs $1,000. Then 15 percent a year is 0.15/365 = 0.000411 a day times twenty days or 0.008219 over twenty days. That is, getting paid twenty days earlier and investing the money would earn interest of 0.8219 percent of $1,000 = $8.22.

So the price can be lowered to $1,000/($1,000.00 + $8.22) = $991.84, a reduction of 8/10 of 1 percent, before the seller is any worse off. That is, $991.84 plus 0.8219 percent of 991.84 = $991.84(1.008219) = $1,000.

The proposal makes little sense because (1) retailers and wholesalers are typically quite sensitive to terms of trade and (2) the reduction in price of 8/10 of 1 percent is too small to be promoted or noticed. Retailers will take the reduction, but they won't change anything. That is, they won't order more or promote more or do anything else for that matter.

12. The figures are all correct. The headings are too, but they are not as clear as they should be. A clearer format and clearer headings would give

	Per Yard			
Suggested retail price	$1.290	100.0%		
Retail gross margin	0.504	39.1		
Wholesale price	0.786	60.9	100.0%	
Wholesale gross margin	0.101		12.8	
Mill net price after discount	0.685		81.2	
Discount				
(@ 7.5% of mill net price)	0.055			7.5
Mill net price	0.740			100.0%

13. Again pick a basis. Assume that normal retail price is 100 and the unknown retail price during the promotion is X. Then we can construct the normal situation and the situation for the price promotion as follows:

		Normal Situation		During Price Promotion	
Price	100	100%		X 100%	
COGS	48	48		38.4	52
Gross margin	52	52		X - 38.4	48

A 20 percent discount from 48 = 48*(0.2) = 9.6, so the COGS during the price promotion is 48 - 9.60 = 38.40.

The gross margin during the promotion is 48 percent, so $(X - 38.4)/X$ must equal 0.48, which means that X is 38.4/0.52 = 73.85. So the discount from normal retail prices is 100 - 73.85 = 26.15, or in round numbers 26 percent.

If your mind is different from mine, you can get the figure by sheer thinking. The discount must be

$$100 - \left(\frac{48 \times 0.8}{52} \times 100 \right) = 100 - 73.85 = 26.15$$

14. The idea makes a lot of sense when the retailer's or wholesaler's income statement is done in percentages. It will be a percentage of sales, not on costs. If gross margins were figured on costs, they wouldn't be comparable

with the rest of the figures.

	Income Statement with Gross Margin as a Percentage of Revenue		*Income Statement with Gross Margin as a Percentage of Cost*	
Sales	$5,000	100%	$5,000	100%
COGS	3,000	60	3,000	60
Gross margin	2,000	40	2,000	67
All expenses	1,800	36	1,800	36
Operating income	200	4	200	4

The second set of figures makes no sense, which is why such figures aren't used.

Chapter 5 - Averages and Marginals– What Marginal Analysis Says

Elementary Problems

1. It is the only way because to raise the average proportion of faculty who are women, the proportion of new hires who are women must be even higher. The marginal must exceed the average. Microeconomists normally make the point with equations. The same point can be made with numbers or with examples.

Numbers

Start with a faculty that is 10 percent women and hire ten new faculty members.

	Faculty at the Start	*Hire 50% Women*	*After- ward*	*Hire 10% Women*	*After- ward*	*Hire No Women*	*After- ward*
Male	90	5	95	9	99	10	100
Female	10	5	15	1	11	--	10
	100	10	110	10	110	10	110
Percentage of women	10%		14%		10%		9%

Example

The soldiers in the Praetorian Guard average six feet tall. To increase their average height, the commander of the guard must recruit guards who are taller than the average.

Like many of the points over which microeconomists labor in the classroom, this one is obvious once it is clearly and simply explained.

2. There is no sure answer to this one. I have uncovered no folk sayings that deal with marginalism. But there must be some. Why are there so few? Perhaps because most people are more comfortable working with totals and averages than with increments. Some microeconomists say it is because marginal analysis is so much a part of the way real people weight costs and benefits that it is too obvious to merit special attention. This is why we have no folk sayings reminding us to breathe every few seconds or not to hold our hand over an open flame.

3. To earn an extra $0.36 the checker takes six or seven seconds, say seven seconds. Then the checker is earning for the store (at the margin) $0.36/7 = $0.0514 per second or $3.09 per minute or $185.14 per hour. If the coupon takes only six seconds to process, the checker earns $214.00 per hour. This is what doesn't ring right. I have no idea what it means.

Slightly More Difficult Problems

Advertising vacant apartments

The line about not needing "budgeting and all that" is of course cockeyed. The real issue is how do you measure marginal value when the revenue is a stream, not a single payment. The formal answer is to discount the stream of rental payments, just as if we were dealing with an annuity. Then marginal analysis would dictate not spending more than the present value of the stream of rental payments. A two-year lease at $900 a month involves cash payments of $900 x 24 = $21,600. Assuming interest rates run 10 percent a year, the present value of a stream of 24 $900-payments is $19,504.

In practice few entrepreneurs (or anyone else outside of the financial sector) could or would do such a computation; and if one were handed to them, they would probably reject its implications. No one in his right mind would spend up to $19,504 to fill an apartment for two years, although at first glance this is what the theory dictates. If one advertised for a while and couldn't fill the apartment, one would lower the rent or add some kind of other financial sweetener or redecorate or whatever. If the apartment didn't rent, the landlord would stop advertising, at least for a while.

The UAW's proposal

(a) The numbers are not correct. The fixed cost per car must go down as the number of cars increases. So the correct figures look like this:

	(millions)		*Per Unit*
Revenues		$2,544	$2,400
Expenses			
Variable	$1,950		$1,840
Fixed	460		434
Total expenses		2,410	2,274
Profit before tax		134	136

where $434 = 460/1.06$. All else is correct. Revenues = $2,544 = $2,400 x 1.06 million cars, and the variable cost per car is total variable cost/Number of cars = $1,950/1.06 million = $1,840.

(b) 1. Revenue is down $100 per car.

2. Costs are also down. Now they are $2,410/1.06 = $2,274. The overhead is spread further. It was $460/1.00 = $460 per car. Now it is $460/1.06 = $434 per car. So total average costs (TAC) are down. TAC now are $434 + $1,840 = $2,274. But the TAC before the price decrease were $2,300/car. So TAC have fallen from $2,300 to $2,274, or $26 per car.

3. So revenue has fallen $100 per car and total average costs have fallen only $26 per car. No wonder profits are down.

You can also see the problem another way, by looking at marginal values. The change in revenue divided by the change in units is (an estimate of) the marginal revenue. The change in total costs divided by the change in units is (an estimate of) the marginal cost.

Marginal Revenue

	Before	*After*	*Change*
Total revenue	2,500	2,544	-44
Number of cars	1	1.06	-0.066
So marginal revenue is			
	-44 / -0.06 =		733

Marginal cost

	Before	*After*	*Change*
Total revenue	2300	2410	-110
Number of cars	1	1.06	-0.06
So marginal cost is			
	-110 / -0.06 =		1833

For this change, the marginal cost exceeds the marginal revenue, which means that you make less after than before the change.

(c) New cars cost around $2,500 in 1955; $2,500 was then equivalent to 34 weeks of income. In 1988, the average cost was $14,000, equivalent to 24 weeks of income. By this measure, cars were a good deal cheaper in 1988. (Source: *MVMA Motor Vehicles Facts & Figures '82*, p. 42 and *MVMA Motor Vehicles Facts & Figures '89*, p. 40.)

Cost of owning a car

Some costs vary with mileage–they are gas, oil, tires, and probably repairs and maintenance. The basic marginal cost is gas at (say) $1.20 a gallon and twenty-five miles a gallon. So gas runs on the order of $1.20/25 = 4.8¢ a mile. Add another two or three or four cents for tires, repairs, and maintenance and you get a variable cost of seven or eight cents.

Other costs do not vary with mileage–insurance, depreciation, registration, taxes, and financing. Here are some order-of-magnitude guesses: insurance $800 a year, depreciation $2,000 a year over seven years, registration $100, taxes $200(?), financing say 12 percent of $10,000 or $1,200 a year. These give a total of $4,300. The AAA estimates that these run around $4,200 a year. (But I knew that before I made my estimates.)

So the order-of-magnitude is that the marginal costs per mile are about one-third or one-fourth of the average costs.

Chapter 6 - The Marketing Control Statement

Elementary Problems

1.

Variable Costs	Varies With	Cost
Manufacturing	Number of units produced	$0.90/unit
Selling factory in dollars	10% of factory sales	
Shipping, breakage, insurance	Number of units stored or shipped	$0.20/unit

Retail price	$10.00	100%	
Retail gross margin	3.33	_33_	
Wholesale price	6.67	67	100%
Wholesale margin	_0.80_		_12_
Manufacturer's price			
(or factory price)	5.87		88

Variable Costs

Manufacturing	$0.90
Shipping	0.20
Selling	_0.59_
	$1.69

(a) Marketing Control Statement for Brand X

		(millions)		*Per Unit*
Revenue (4.8m units @$5.87)		$28.18	100%	$5.87
Variable cost @$1.69		_8.11_	_29_	_1.69_
Gross marketing contribution		$20.07	71	4.18
Programmed marketing				
Advertising	2.40			
Brand management	_.35_	_2.75_	_10_	
Net marketing contribution		17.32	61	

(b) The unit GMC is $4.18.

(c) To just cover programmed marketing expenses, sales must be $2.75m + $4.18 = 0.66m units, or 3.3 percent of the current market (m =

millions).

(d) Since 3.3 percent of the market is worth $20.07m, the value of a share point is $20.07/3.3 = $6.08m.

(e) Proposed programmed marketing costs are $5m plus $0.35m. To just cover these costs sales must be $5.35m + $4.18 = 1.28m units.

(f) To cover the proposed programmed marketing costs and produce $17.31m in net marketing contribution, sales must be ($5.35m + $17.31m) + $4.18 = 5.42m units, or 24 percent of next year's market.

(g) 5.42m units is 24 percent of next year's market.

(h) To cover produced programmed marketing costs and produce $21m in net marketing contribution, sales must be ($5.35m + $21m) + $4.18 = 6.3m units or 27 percent of next year's market.

2. Return to your answer to the Wendy's problem in Chapter 3, separate costs into three groups–variable, programmed marketing expenses, and all other– and discard all other. Students' answers will vary according to their judgments as to what is variable and what isn't.

The variable costs are:

Crew	10.0%
Food	39.0
Paper	3.4
Laundry	.2
Payroll taxes	2.0
Royalty	4.0
Supplies and uniforms	1.6

Advertising is a question mark. Is it programmed or variable? The question doesn't say. (In fact, at Wendy's it is variable.)

So there are two possible MCSs.

	Advertising Variable		*Advertising Programmed*
Sales	100.0%		100.0%
Variable costs			
excluding advertising	60.2	60.2	
Advertising	4.0	64.2	–	60.2
GMC	35.8		39.8
Programmed			
Advertising		4.0	
NMC	35.8		35.8

Note that treating advertising as programmed at 4 percent looks like a programmed cost is being treated as variable. Not so. This is simply a way of getting a ballpark figure. If sales were to increase, for example, programmed advertising would not–or need not–change, and it would therefore no longer be 4 percent of sales. This is another obvious point, but some students and some managers mulishly think that 4 percent of sales means 4 percent of sales, no matter what sales are.

3. Revenues

			(millions)
Fees			
Number of cards (m)	5.1		
Annual fee	$15	$ 76.5	
Interest			
Number of cards(m)	5.1		
Average balance	$1,300		
Interest	18.9%	$1,253.1	
Merchant charges			
Number of cards (m)	5.1		
Average billing/card	$1,166		
Discount	2.6%	$ 154.6	
Total revenues			$1,484.2
Variable costs			
Borrowed money			
Interest paid	8.0%		
Number of cards (m)	5.1		
Average billing/card	$1,166	$ 475.7	
Bad debts			
Bad debt rate	3.6%		
Number of cards (m)	5.1		
Average balance	$1,300	$ 238.7	
Total variable costs			$ 714.4

Gross marketing contribution		$ 769.8

Programmed costs
Advertising	$ 23.0	
Sales force	47.0	
All other	6.7	
Total programmed costs		$ 76.7

| Net marketing contribution | | $ 693.1 |

4. PDQ Systems

(a) $12.75 + $11.4 = $24.15 million. Advertising and the sales force are programmed costs.

(b) Variable costs are $775 + 50 = $825 per unit.

(c) Contribution per unit.

Retail price	$2,000		100%	
Distributors' combined margins		700		35
Manufacturer's selling price	1,300		65	
Variable costs	825			
Unit contribution	475			

(d) To just cover programmed marketing costs PDQ must sell $6,250,000/475 = 13,158 units. To just cover programmed marketing costs, fixed costs, and overhead: 6,250,000 + 24,150,000 = $30.4 million/475 = 64,000 units.

(e) PDQ sells 75,000 units and has eleven share points. The total market is therefore 75,000/0.11 = 682,000. To break even, PDQ needs a share of 64,000/682,000 = 9 percent.

(f)
Revenues 75,000 units @ $1,300		$97,500
Variable costs		
Production + shipping = $825/unit x 75,000		61,875
Gross marketing contribution		35,625
Programmed marketing expense		
Advertising	1,950	
Sales force	4,300	6,250
Net marketing contribution		29,375
All other costs $12,750 + $11,400		24,150
Net income		$ 5,225

(g) & (h) Raise the ad budget by 20 percent or by 0.2 x $1.95 million = $390,000. To just cover the extra advertising, PDQ must sell an extra 390,000/475 = 821 printers. Compson expects sales to increase by 1 to 2 percent. A 1 percent increase is 750, a 2 percent increase is 1,500. So the extra advertising may not pay its way.

(i) Two cartridges will cost $87.50 x 2 = $175 and lower the unit contribution from $475 to $300. Then the number of extra units needed to just cover the extra $390,000 in advertising would be 390,000/300 = 1,300 units, or 1,300/682,000 = 0.2 of a share point. Since Compson expected sales to increase by 1 to 2 percent with the advertising alone, this looks like a safe bet.

Slightly More Difficult Problems

New York State Lottery

Assume gross receipts of 100. Then the MCS looks like this

	At 5%		At 10%	
Receipts		100		X
Variable Costs				
Commissions	5		0.1X	
Prizes	30	35	0.3X	0.4X
GMC	65		0.6X	

We want 0.6X to equal 65, so X = 108.3. That is, if the commission to retailers is doubled, sales must increase by 8.3 percent to leave the lottery as well off as before (in GMC or in NMC).

If the commission increases from 5 to 7 percent, the sales increase needed is 3.2 percent.

Life Cereal

1. Get the factory price:

	Per case	
Retail price	$5.60	100%
Retail gross margin	0.98	17.5
Factory price	4.62	82.5

2. Use 39.6 percent as an estimate of variable cost.

Factory price	$4.62	100%
Estimated variable cost	1.83	39.6
Gross marketing contribution	2.79	60.4

3. The number of cases sold must be

$$\frac{\text{Sales at factory}}{\text{Factory price/case}} = \frac{\$2.7 \text{ million}}{\$4.62/\text{case}}$$

$$= 584,000 \text{ cases (rounding)}$$

4. The marketing control statement for Life is

	In millions	Per Case
Sales	$2.70	$4.62
Variable costs	1.07	1.83
Gross marketing contribution	1.63	2.79
Programmed costs		
Advertising @ 8 percent 0.22		
Sales force @ 3.5 percent 0.09		
Research @ .5 percent 0.01		
Net marketing contribution	$1.31	

5. The proposal involves an increase in the ad budget of $345,000 - 220,000 = $125,000. With the sampling scheme, the total increase is $125,000 + 135,000 = $260,000. To just cover the added $260,000, Life must sell

$$\frac{260,000}{2.79} = 93,000 \text{ more cases}$$

6. Life has 1.4 percent of the market by weight. It sells (around) 584,000 cases each weighing 24 boxes x (10 oz/16) = 15 lb, for a total of 584,000 x 15 = 8.76 million pounds.

If 1.4 percent is 8.76 million pounds, then the entire market must be 8.76/0.014 = 625.7 million pounds.

In terms of the overall market the break-even cases are

$$\frac{93,000 \times 15 \text{ lb}}{625.7 \text{ million}} = 2/10 \text{ of } 1 \text{ percent of the market.}$$

or 0.2 of one share point.

Hot Dog Man

Note that there are some guesses below.

Louie during the Summer

Sales		Per Day
100 hot dogs @ $1		$100.00
75 sodas @ $.75		56.25
10 sausages @ $1		10.00
20 knishes @ $.75		15.00
Total sales		$181.25

Variable costs		
100 hot dogs @ 7 per $2.50	$ 35.71	
75 sodas @ 24 for $8	25.00	
10 sausages @ 6 for $2.35	3.92	
20 knishes @ 30 per $9.75	6.50	
Propane @ $12 per week	2.40	
Ice	40.00	
Straws, onions, ketchup, and napkins (guess)	15.00	
Total variable costs		$128.53
Gross marketing contribution		52.72

Louie Per Year

Say Louie works five days a week, fifty weeks a year, of which sixteen are summer weeks and thirty-four are winter weeks.

Summer GMC = $52.72 x 5 x 16	$4,217.60	
Winter GMC = $52.72 x (1/2) x 5 x 34	4,481.20	
Total GMC per year		$8,698.80
Capacity and other costs on an annual basis		
A cart costs $4,500 and lasts five years	900.00	
Garage @ 12 x $275	3,300.00	
Occasional repairs (a guess)	300.00	
Fines–a couple @ $1,000 each over 5? years	400.00	
	4,900.00	
Net marketing contribution before other carts		3,798.80
Net income from his five other carts		
Summer: 5 x (52.72-40)/2 x 5 x 16		2,544.00
Winter: none because winter profits are below $40/day		
Annual income before taxes		$6,342.80

The conclusion is that something is wrong. Louie won't work that hard for $6,300 a year. The journalist didn't check his figures (which is no surprise) so the figures may be off. Perhaps Louie didn't want to look too wealthy so he shaded the figures. Perhaps ...

Testing Price

Start by computing the total GMC at each of the four prices. Ignore the 13.5 percent because it is clearly not a variable cost. You get

Price	$359.00	$329.00	$299.00	$269.00
Variable cost	151.30	151.30	151.30	151.30
Customs	7.57	7.57	7.57	7.57
Total variable cost	158.87	158.87	158.87	158.87
Unit GMC	$200.13	$170.13	$140.13	$110.13
Units sold	107	213	201	410
Total GMC	$21,414	$36,238	$28,166	$45,153

What to do? If there is no time, price at $269 or lower. If there is time for another test, try still lower prices because (1) the total GMC is still going up at $269 and (2) many students should know that $250 or so is a very competitive price. So trying even lower prices makes some sense.

If prices are lowered even more, here is what unit sales must be to beat $45,155.

At a price of	$249	$229	$199
Unit sales must be	501	644	1,125

Whether this is likely enough to continue testing is a judgment call.

Note that if the student erroneously includes the 13.5 percent, he comes to the same conclusions. The variable cost then becomes $151.30 + 5 percent + 13.5% = $179.29, and the total GMC become $19,229, $31,888, $24,062, and $36,781. So much for clean living and doing what teacher says.

Video Tapes

First calculate the skim wholesale price. The list price of $89.95 and a GM of 28 percent imply a wholesale price of $64.76. Use $65.

The wholesale price at the end of the decade ran around $15.50. So the variable cost is probably (say) one-third of $15.50 or $5.00. Then

	Skim	Penetration
Wholesale price	$65	$15
Variable cost	5	5
Unit GMC	60	10

As long as penetration sales are at least six times greater than skim sales, the studios earn a higher GMC. The question says that penetration sales ran several million while skim sales ran several hundred thousand. So on this rough qualitative scale, it looks like penetration sales are indeed six times greater.

See figures in the answer to the last question for Chapter 4.

Direct Mail Promotion

As always with these problems, there is some guessing involved as to which costs are variable and which are allocations of non-variable costs. Here are my guesses: the variable costs are merchandise, royalties, order processing, United Parcel Service (UPS), premiums, and taxes. The rest are simply allocations of programmed costs or overhead costs.

Thus, the MCS would be

Total selling price		$38.90
Variable costs		
Merchandise	$14.35	
Royalties	0.22	
Order processing	2.30	
UPS	2.25	
Taxes	.25	19.37
GMC per order		19.53

The program at issue is, say, a catalog mailing or a direct response advertisement.

The Direct Mail Worksheet:

There is nothing particularly deep in this problem. It is simply messy, and students rarely come up with the figures below. As in other examples, I chose to work with a basis, in this case, a basis that assumes 100,000 units shipped. The following figures should speak for themselves.

Work with a basis of 100,000 units

Gross units shipped   100,000
    Less: returns @ 8.20 percent   8,200
Net units shipped   91,800

R e v e n u e s

Category	Percent	Number of Units	Revenue per Unit	Total Revenue	
Don't Pay	1.09%	1,001	$ 0		
Pay	98.91	90,799	38.90	$3,532,081	
Total revenues	100.00	91,800		3,532,096	$3,532,081

C o s t s

I. Variable costs of shipping 100,000 units
    Order processing $ 2.30
    United Parcel   2.25
    Total variable
      shipping costs $ 4.55 x 100,000 units shipped $ 455,000

II. Variable cost of sales of 91,800 units
    Merchandise $14.35
    Royalties   0.22
    Taxes   0.25
    Total variable
      cost of sales $14.82 x 91,800 units sold   1,360,476

III. Cost of returns
    Postage and
      handling $ 2.46
    Cleaning   1.13
    Total cost
      of returns $ 3.59 x 8,200 units returned   29,438

Total variable costs of shipping 100,000 units,
    selling 91,800 and handling returns of 8,200 $1,844,914

Gross marketing contribution $1,687,167

    Average GMC per unit shipped = $1,687,167/100,000 = $16.87
    Average GMC per unit sold   = $1,687,167/ 91,800 = $18.38

Comments on the Direct Mail Worksheet:

1. The GMC per unit sold is the key figure. It gives you the unit contribution

after adjustments for bad debts and returns, after all the dust has settled, so to speak.

2. Are bad debts and returns in fact variable costs? Yes. A direct mailer would expect bad debts and returns to increase in proportion to units shipped.

3. Everything is straightforward to V. Expected Returns Cost. So let us start there.

    V.   The average cost of returns per unit shipped is 29,438/100,000 = $0.29, the figure given. It is truly an <u>expected value</u>.

    VI.   Given, except for one ambiguity. Is it 1.09 percent of items shipped or 1.09 percent of items sold? Since you can't have bad debts until you sell something, it must be 1.09 percent of items sold.

    VII.   Another expected value, which does not appear above because I never counted the revenue from these in the first place. But the worksheet does. So it has to be backed out from revenue initially recognized.

    VIII.   This is the sum of the three numbers above it:

$$\$21.45 + 0.29 + 0.43 = \$22.17$$

    IX.   Here the worksheet is preparing to do another expected value calculation, this time on those items sold (i.e., shipments net of returns).

    X.   This is an expected value. The average cost of a sale after adjusting for returns (via IX) and bad debts (via VII).

    XI.   This is revenue per sale less expected variable cost per sale. So it is a unit contribution.

    XII.   This is backed out of the variable cost an adjustment for returned merchandise.

    XIII.   This purports to be an average contribution per unit sold after adjusting for both bad debts and returns, but it isn't because it includes an allocation of fixed costs.

Silvermark Products, Inc.

Here are the unit GMCs.

	Manufacturers' Selling Price	Variable Cost per Unit	GMC Cost per Unit
Deluxe	$125.00	$47.00	$78.00
Standard	70.00	30.00	40.00
Thrift	45.00	22.00	23.00
GetMor	55.00	26.00	29.00
GetMor Plus	36.00	18.00	18.00

Add a private label?

	No	Yes	Cannibalization Rate
Deluxe	3,000	2,940	2%
Standard	11,385	9,108	20
Thrift	17,595	13,196	25
GetMor		8,000	
GetMor Plus	_____	_3,500_	
Unit sales	31,980	36,744	

Notes: 1. 3,000 + no growth = 3,000 less 2 percent cannibalization = 2,940 units per month.
2. 11,000 + 3.5 percent growth = 11,385 less 20 percent cannibalization = 9,108 units per month.

Pro Forma Marketing Control Statement

	No	Yes		
Total GMC	$1,094,085	$1,192,154		
Programmed costs	_500,000_	_500,000_		
Total NMC	$ 594,085	$ 692,154	14.2%	increase in NMC before tooling
One-time costs		_55,000_		
NMC after one-time costs		$ 637,154	7.2%	increase in NMC after tooling

Note: $1,094,085 = 3,000(78) + 11,385(40) + 17,595(23)$

Based on the numbers alone, the private label will increase NMC by 14 percent before tooling, 7 percent after tooling. Since (1) the tooling is a direct, avoidable cost, and (2) the contract is basically on a year-to-year basis, tooling must be considered, and the 7 percent figure is the one to use. Hence the idea should be dropped.

With the figures this close, and the Alabama plant forecast to run at less than capacity for the next year or two, SP management should talk to the chain again to see if it can work out a better deal.

No deal of this importance can be decided on the figures alone. Does SP want to do private label? Is there much risk that after SP has taken the private label contract, the Alabama plant will have to turn away more profitable business? Will making private label mixers make it harder in a slow growth market for SP to get full price for its own brands?

Chapter 7 - Break-even and Just Cover Points

Elementary Problems

1. Normal sales are 160 items a month, which is 160 items every 4 weeks, or 240 items in 6 weeks.

    The formula gives us as the just cover increase in sales

    $$\frac{55 - 41.80}{41.80} = 32\%$$

    So sales have to increase from 240 to 240(1.32) = 316

    Some figure that a month contains 52/12 = 4.33 weeks, in which case normal sales during a six-week period would be 222 items, and sales then would have to increase to 293 items to just cover the previous retail gross margin.

2. The contribution per pair of shoes is $23.40 less another 8 percent of 78.00 = 23.40 - 6.24 = $17.16. Therefore, to just cover annual expenses the new outlet must sell $710,000/$17.16 = 41,000 pairs.

    The exact member is $710,000/$17.16 = 41,375.29. This might be the time to discuss the false accuracy implied by 41,375.29 pairs of shoes.

3.

	Now	With $0.06 Reduction	With $0.12 Reduction
Price	$0.75	$0.69	$0.63
Variable Cost	_0.083_	_0.083_	_0.083_
GMC/pound	0.667	0.607	0.547

So to just cover the $0.06 reduction sales must increase $(0.667 - 0.607)/0.607 = 0.06/0.607 = 9.9$ percent, and $0.06/0.547 = 11$ percent for the $0.12 reduction.

4. The figures imply an average gross margin of $435,000/2.4$ million $= 18.1$ percent. So the MCS at break-even is

Sales	$2,400	100.0%
COGS	_1.965_	_81.9_
GMC	435	18.1
Overhead	_435_	
Bottom line	0	

Slightly More Difficult Problems

District of Columbia Lottery

The major issue is how much gross receipts must increase to leave the board with the same gross marketing contribution as it earned in 1983. Let GR stand for the unknown gross receipts. Prizes are a variable cost, by common sense; contract services are by the statement in the footnote. Both vary with gross receipts, not net receipts; hence we take percentages on gross receipts.

	Current MCS		MCS with a 10% Agent fee
Gross receipts	$54,071	100.0	GR
Agents' fees	_3.388_	_6.3_	0.1 GR
Net receipts	$50,683	93.7%	0.9 GR
Prizes	26,858	49.7	
Contract services	_9.863_	_18.2_	
Total variable costs	_36.721_	_67.9_	0.679GR
GMC	13,962	25.8%	0.9GR - 0.679GR

GMC $= \$13{,}962 = 0.9$GR $- 0.679$GR, so GR $= \$63{,}176$, an increase of around 17 percent.

Cosmair

The only problem with this one is the break in the group sales bonus at $13 million. It makes the problem messy, but that's all. The problem presents no intellectual difficulties.

Note that product overhead is most likely a mixture of fixed and programmed costs. But the problem doesn't say what the mixture is.

The district manager will certainly consider product overhead a variable cost, and correctly, from his point of view. But the people making the decision are in New York. They (and we) can see that product overhead is not variable. So leave it out of the calculations.

Pro Forma MCS for District #17 before Extra Advertising
(millions)

Sales	$10.85	100.0%	
Variable costs			
Labor	$1.59		14.7
Materials	3.27		30.1
Sales commissions	0.38		3.5
Sales bonus–up to $13 million	0.05		0.5
Sales bonus–over $13 million			
Total variable costs		5.29	48.8
Gross marketing contribution		5.56	51.2
Programmed marketing costs		--	
Net marketing contribution		5.56	

The problem is to find the sales that will give $5.56m NMC after spending $1.6m for extra advertising. The answer is sales of $14.03m.

(all figures in millions except 0.512)

$13.00	Maximum sales allowed at lower sales, bonus
$10.85	Sales forecast
$ 2.15	Maximum extra sales allowed at lower sales bonus
x 0.512	GMC percentage at lower sales bonus
$ 1.10	Extra GMC available to pay off extra advertising
$ 1.60	Extra advertising
1.10	Portion paid when sales increase to $13m as above
0.50	Remaining advertising to be covered at the higher sales bonus

51.2%	GMC percentage under lower bonus
2.5%	Extra bonus for sales over $13m
48.7%	GMC percentage under higher bonus, that is when sales are over $13m

$$\frac{0.50m}{0.487} = 1.027$$ Sales above $13m needed to pay remaining $0.59m in advertising.

Round 1.027 to 1.03. Then the total sales needed to just cover the extra $1.6m is 13 + 1.03 = $14.03m. The complete MCS follows.

No Hassle Treatment of Complaints

Costs	Monthly Costs
Investigate 1,000 complaints @ $45 each	$ 45,000
Pay 950 refunds @ $135 each	128,250
Total	173,250

Therefore we can pay without investigation $173,250/1,000 = $173 per complaint and be no worse off. If we continue to pay $135, the complaints department can cut its expenses by $38,000:

What we pay now	$173,250
Less: What we would pay if we simply paid out $135 each	135,000
Savings	38,250

Since there is no obvious reason to pay more than $135, the savings should run around $38,000 a month (plus savings that come from avoiding investigation costs).

Pro Forma MCS for District #17 to Just Cover the Extra Advertising
(millions)

	Up to $13 m a		Above $13m b		Total a+b	
Sales	$13.00	100.0%	$1.03	100.0%	$14.03	100.0%
Variable Costs						
Labor	$1.91	14.7	$0.15	14.7	$2.06	14.7
Materials	3.91	30.1	0.31	30.1	4.22	30.1
Sales commissions	0.46	3.5	0.04	3.5	0.49	3.5
Sales bonus–0.5 of 1% up to $13	0.07	0.5			0.07	0.5
Sales bonus–3% over $13			0.03	3.0	0.03	0.2
Total variable costs	6.34	48.8	0.53	51.3	6.87	49.0
Gross marketing contribution	6.66	51.2	0.50	48.7	7.16	51.0
Programmed marketing costs						
Extra advertising					1.60	
Net marketing contribution	6.66		0.50		5.56	

Index

About the Author

DAVID L. RADOS is Professor of Marketing at the Owen Graduate School of Management, Vanderbilt University. He has taught graduate students at Harvard, Columbia, and Vanderbilt and at universities in Australia, Tanzania, and England. He is a popular speaker and has run successful executive seminars for clients and universities on three continents for over twenty years. He has written three books, including the best-selling book *Marketing for Non-Profit Organizations* (Auburn House, 1981), and many articles on marketing. He has consulted for such companies as Scott Paper, AT&T, the Girl Scouts of America, and the New York Port Authority. He has served as a director of a machine equipment company and an expert witness in patent litigation.